ON THE DEFICIDENCIES

IN THE

PRESENT ADMINISTRATION OF HINDU LAW

ON THE DEFICIDENCIES

IN THE

PRESENT ADMINISTRATION OF HINDU LAW

BEING

A PAPER

READ AT THE MEETING OF THE EAST INDIA ASSOCIATION ON THE 8TH OF, JUNE, 1870

THEODORE GOLDSTUCKER

GYAN

Published by

GYAN

Gyan Publishing House
5, Ansari Road
Daryaganj, New Delhi-110002
Phone: 011-47034999, 9811692060
E-mail: books@gyanbooks.com

Distribution Network
gyanbooks.com
India, USA, Canada, UK, Australia

ISBN: 978-93-7097-410-4 (HB)
First Published, 1871

2nd Impression 2025

Printed at: Gyan Press, Delhi.

ON THE DEFICIDENCIES IN THE PRESENT ADMINISTRATION OF HINDU LAW

Author: THEODORE GOLDSTUCKER

ON THE DEFICIENCIES

IN THE

PRESENT ADMINISTRATION OF HINDU LAW;

BEING

A PAPER

READ AT THE MEETING OF THE EAST INDIA ASSOCIATION ON THE 8TH OF JUNE, 1870,

BY

TH. GOLDSTÜCKER,

PROFESSOR OF SANSKRIT IN UNIVERSITY COLLEGE, LONDON, ETC.

1871.

ON THE DEFICIENCIES

IN THE

PRESENT ADMINISTRATION OF HINDU LAW.

THE attention of the East India Association having lately been drawn by Mr. W. Tayler to some urgent wants in the administration of justice, in so far as Indian litigants in general are concerned, it may not be inexpedient to bring under your notice the difficulties which beset the course of justice in reference to a particular class of cases which it did not enter into the scope of Mr. Tayler's able paper to deal with, viz. of those cases which are governed by Hindu law.

This law, I need not explain, concerns two topics of litigation only—that of inheritance and that of adoption — topics intimately connected with Hindu religious belief, and therefore allowed to remain free from the touch of foreign legislation.

The Hindu law, it is likewise unnecessary for me to add, is laid down in the ancient and mediæval works of the Hindus, all of which are written in Sanskrit. It is contained in the code of Manu, in that of Yâjña-valkya, in the codes of numerous legislators, which are intermediate between, or posterior to, both these great authorities, and in a number of subsequent, but very important commentaries and digests, which have developed the ancient law, and ultimately, because latest in time, have become first in authority.* Amongst these, one of the most important in all matters relating to the law of inheritance is the *Mitâksharâ* of *Vijñâneśvara*, which, as Colebrooke says, is, with the exception of Bengal, "received in all the schools of Hindu law, from Benares to the southern

* See 'Yâjñavalkya-Dharmaśâstra,' I., 4, 5; H. T. Colebrooke's Preface to 'Two Treatises on the Hindu Law of Inheritance;' A. F. Stenzler, "Zur Literatur der Indischen Gesetzbücher," in A. Weber's 'Indische Studien,' vol. i., pp. 232 ff.; Standish Grove Grady, 'A Treatise on the Hindoo Law of Inheritance,' pp. lix.–lxxiv.

extremity of the peninsula of India, as the chief groundwork of the doctrines which they follow, and as an authority from which they rarely dissent."* The Mitâksharâ was expanded in subsequent digests, and, in consequence, the Vivâdachintâmańi, the Ratnâkara, and Vivâdachandra, became the first legal authorities, on matters of inheritance, in Mithilâ (Tirhut); the Vîramitrodaya and the works of Kamalâkara became so at Benares; the Vyavahâramayûkha amongst the Mahrattas, and the Smŕitichandrikâ and Vyavahâra-Mâdhavîya at Madras.

In Bengal the paramount authority on the law of inheritance is Jîmûtavâhana's Dâyabhâga, which in several important respects differs from the ruling of the Mitâksharâ; and in agreement with it are Raghunandana's Dâyatattva, Śrîkŕishńa-Tarkâlamkâra's Dâyakramasamgraha, besides various other works, which it is not necessary here to enumerate.†

The best authorities on the law of adoption are the Dattakamîmâmsâ, by Nanda Pańdita; the Dattakachandrikâ, by Devańda Bhaťťa; and after them, the Dattakanirńaya, Dattakatilaka, Dattakadarpańa, Dattakakaumudî, Dattakadîdhiti, and Dattakasiddhântamañjarî. All these commentaries and digests derive their authority from, and profess to be based on, the codes of Manu and Yâjñavalkya and the other lawgivers already alluded to. They do not admit that there is any real difference between the laws laid down in the ancient works; and wherever any such differences seem to exist, they either endeavour to reconcile them by the interpretations they put on their texts, or explain them away by the assumption of accidental omissions which they supply. And it is in consequence of such interpretations or additions that different conclusions have obtained in the Mitâksharâ- and the Bengal-schools, though both profess to derive their opinions from a correct and authoritative understanding of the same ancient texts.

That all these commentaries and digests, whenever it suits their line of argument, occasionally also refer to other non-legal works of Sanskrit literature, such as the vedic Gŕihyasûtras, the Mahâbhârata, Râmâyańa, the Purâńas, and even the grammar of Pâńini, need not surprise us, for their object is to convey the impression that a harmonious spirit pervades the whole antiquity of India, and that their ruling, therefore, is in accordance with all that is sacred to the Hindu mind.

Now, from the facts I have been able to gather, it would appear that, with scarcely any exception, the English judges who are entrusted with the administration of the Hindu law of inheritance and adoption, are not

---

* 'Two Treatises,' Pref., p. iv.

† Compare the works mentioned in the note of the preceding page.

acquainted with the Sanskrit language, and are unable therefore to found their decisions on a direct and immediate knowledge and examination of the original law sources just mentioned. They must resort, therefore, to second-hand information which they derive from translations, and the assistance afforded them by the pleadings of counsel and otherwise. But as I am probably not very wrong in assuming that for the most part the counsel, too, are indebted for their knowledge of the Hindu law, not to the original texts, but to translations of them, these translations are the real basis on which the administration of the Hindu law at present rests, and it will, therefore, be necessary to give a brief account of them.

Of the code of Manu there exists the well-known complete translation of Sir W. Jones, first published in 1794, then in 1796, and reprinted by Haughton in 1825. It was translated into German by Hüttner in 1797. A French translation of the original by Loiseleur Deslongchamps, mainly agreeing with that of his celebrated predecessor, appeared in 1833.* A complete translation in German of the code of Yâjñavalkya was published by Professor Stenzler in 1849; and some portions of the same code translated into English by Dr. Roer and Mr. Montriou appeared in 1859.

The Mitâksharâ of Vijñâneśvara is a running commentary on each verse of Yâjñavalkya's Institutes. The latter consist of three parts. The first treats of *âchâra*, or established rules of conduct, comprising such

* About thirty years ago, I believe, there appeared at Calcutta a few parts of a new edition and translation of Manu, which seem to have remained almost unknown in Europe. The quarto volume in question, when opened, contains on the left side in one column the text of Manu in Devanâgarî, and in Bengali characters; and in another, a Bengali translation of the corresponding verses, a few foot-notes in Bengali being generally added to the page; on the right side it contains in one column Sir W. Jones's translation, and parallel to it, in another column, a new English translation, which may be looked upon as a running criticism on the former. For though it repeats as much as it approves of Sir W. Jones's translation, in the very words of the latter, this is apparently done in order to make its divergence from it still more prominent; and this divergence is not inconsiderable, and very often marks a decided improvement on the rendering of Sir W. Jones. Foot-notes in English, moreover, are frequently added to justify the discrepancies. Unfortunately—for there is no doubt that the author of the new translation was a very competent scholar—in the two copies of it known to me, the text breaks off at verse 40, and the translation at verse 33, of Book 3, while these two copies do not contain the name of the author or a date; and since all my endeavours to learn more about the progress of the work have been unsuccessful, I apprehend that no more of it, than the portions I have seen, has appeared in print. The name of the editor and translator, as I learn from a friend, is Tarachund Chuckerbutt.

subjects as education and marriage, funeral rites, &c. The second part treats of *vyavahâra*, or the business of life, including amongst many other topics judicature and inheritance; the third part treats of *prâyaśchitta*, and comprises penance, purification, transmigration, and kindred subjects. Of the Vyavahâra part of the Mitâksharâ eight chapters translated by W. H. Macnaghten first appeared in 1829; and that portion of it which strictly relates to inheritance, about the fourteenth part of the whole work, exists in the well-known translation by Colebrooke, first published in 1810, and then edited in his Hindu law books by Mr. Whitley Stokes in 1865. Of the Vyavahâramayûkha, Harry Borradaile published a translation in 1827, which likewise reappeared in Mr. Stokes's Hindu law books in 1865.

The Vivâdachintâmaṅi, translated into English by Prossonno Coomar Tagore, was published in 1863; the Vyavahâra-Mâdhavîya, by Mr. A. C. Burnell, in 1868, and—through the medium of Tamul sources, as I am informed—the Smṛitichandrikâ, by Mr. T. Kristnasawmy Iyer, in 1867. Of Jîmûtavâhana's Dâyabhâga we possess the translation of Colebrooke, first published in 1810, and in his law books by Mr. Stokes in 1865; and of the Dâyakramasaṁgraha—also edited in the same collection by the same distinguished scholar—the translation of Wynch, first published in 1818.

Lastly, the Dattakamîmâṁsâ and Dattakachandrikâ exist in a translation by Sutherland, first published in 1821, then in 1825, and also embodied in Mr. Stokes's Hindu law books.

Besides these few translations, nothing whatever worth mentioning, out of the large bulk of Hindu law literature, is accessible to the English judge, if unacquainted with Sanskrit, except a few disconnected verses of the ancient lawgivers, put together, without any reference to the context in which they stand, in the Digest of Hindu law prepared by Jagannâtha under the directions of Sir W. Jones.*

The question, then, which I have to raise is this: Do these translations—a mere fraction, I need not say, of the large mass of Hindu

* Colebrooke's opinion of this Digest is contained in the following passage from his preface to the 'Two Treatises,' &c., p. ii.:—"In the preface to the translation of the Digest, I hinted an opinion unfavorable to the arrangement of it, as it has been executed by the native compiler. I have been confirmed in that opinion of the compilation, since its publication; and indeed the author's method of discussing together the discordant opinions maintained by the lawyers of the several schools, without distinguishing in an intelligible manner which of them is the received doctrine of each school, but on the contrary leaving it uncertain whether any of the opinions stated by him do actually prevail, or which doctrine must now be considered to be in force and which obsolete,

law literature — suffice both in quality and quantity for ensuring to litigants a proper and satisfactory administration of the Hindu law of inheritance and adoption?

Before giving my opinion on this point, I will place myself in the position of a judge who has no means of examining for himself the original text of a statute, and I should then have to assume that the question asked must be answered by him in the affirmative. For on what grounds could he decide that the translations enumerated above were insufficient in quantity, and how could he undertake to say that any objection mooted against their reliability was valid or not? It would be a dangerous and, I hold, an arbitrary proceeding on his part were he to overrule, for instance, the translation of a passage by Tagore or Burnell, merely because the translation of the same passage by Colebrooke did not agree with it, and because the authority of Colebrooke stands higher than that of the scholars differing from him. For however high the authority of anyone, a doubt of this kind cannot be finally settled by it; and a mere consideration of the immense progress made by Sanskrit studies since the time when the great Colebrooke wrote, of the large quantity of new materials that have since come to light, of all the advantages in short, which, in consequence of the very labours of Colebrooke, later workers in the same field must have over him, would naturally make a judge hesitate in disposing of such doubts simply on the ground of tradition and authority.

Yet instances of such conflicting translations are by no means rare; and where therefore for his final opinion the judge would have to rely on third parties, his position would at any rate not be safe.

To illustrate this uncertainty I will choose at random a few examples as they occur to me.

The Mitâksharâ and the digests, as I have already observed, constantly support their statements by quotations from Manu, Yâjñavalkya, and the other lawgivers; but as every disputed case has not been foreseen by them, these very quotations sometimes become the principal basis on which the judgment in a particular case has to rest.

In dealing with the rights of brothers, a verse of Yâjñavalkya is quoted by the Dâyabhâga of Jîmûtavâhana, which Colebrooke translates as follows:—

"A half-brother, being again associated, may take the succession; not

---

renders his work of little utility to persons conversant with the law, and of still less service to those who are not versed in *Indian* jurisprudence; especially to the *English* reader, for whose use, through the medium of translation, the work was particularly intended."

a *half-brother,** though not re-united: but one united [by blood, *though not by coparcenery*] may obtain the property; and not [*exclusively*] the son of a different mother."†

In the Vivâdachintâmańi, Tagore translates this verse thus:—

"Re-united step-brothers, but not *brothers* who live separated, shall take each other's property. A uterine brother *even when he is separated*, shall have the property. But a *separated* step-brother cannot get it."‡

Again, in the Vyavahâramayûkha we find Borradaile translating this verse:—

"One of a different womb, being again associated, may take the succession; not one of a different womb, if not re-united: but [a whole brother *if*] *re-united*, obtains the property; and not [*exclusively*] the son of a different mother."§

Hence, according to Colebrooke a brother united by blood; according to Tagore, a uterine brother, *even when he is separated*, may obtain the property; while according to Borradaile a whole brother may obtain it, but only on the condition of being *re-united*. Again, Colebrooke and Borradaile say that the son of a different mother cannot get the succession *exclusively*, while Tagore says, that a step-brother cannot get it, if *separated*.

Or, under the heading of effects not liable to partition, the Mitâksharâ cites a verse from Nârada, which Colebrooke translates:—

"He who maintains the family of a brother studying science, shall take, be he ever so ignorant, a share of the wealth gained by science." ‖

In the Vyavahâra-Mâdhavîya, Mr. Burnell renders the same verse:—

"A member of a family though he be ignorant, who supports his brother while learning science, shall get a share of the wealth acquired by that brother by learning."¶

And Tagore, in the Vivâdachintâmańi:—

"Wealth, acquired by a learned man, whose family was supported, *during his absence from home* to acquire learning, by a brother, shall be shared with the latter, even if he be ignorant."**

Hence, according to Tagore's version a brother acquires this right only when he supports his brother's family during his absence from home—a restriction not contained in Colebrooke's and Burnell's translation of the same passage.

---

* The *italics* in this and the following quotations are intended to facilitate a comparison of the discrepancies.

† XI., 5, 13. ‡ P. 306. § IV., 9, 10. ‖ I., 4, 8.
¶ P. 49. ** P. 253.

Again, when treating of the succession to a woman's peculiar property, Jîmûtavâhana's Dâyabhâga quotes a verse of Devala, which according to Colebrooke says:—

"Her subsistence, her ornaments, her perquisite, and *her gains*, are the separate property of a woman. She herself exclusively enjoys it; and her husband has no right to use it, unless in distress."*

But in the Vivâdachintâmańi, Tagore renders the same verse thus:—

"Food and vesture, ornaments, perquisites, and *wealth received by a woman from a kinsman*, are her own property;" &c.†

Hence, in Colebrooke's translation the *strídhana* applies to all the gains of a woman; while in that of Tagore—and he italicizes the words "from a kinsman"—it applies solely to the wealth which a woman receives *from a kinsman*.

The word perquisite (sometimes also called "fee") in the foregoing quotations is the Sanskrit *śulka*, and as an item of *strídhana* it is defined in Jîmûtavâhana's Dâyabhâga by a reference to Kâtyâyana, which Colebrooke translates as follows:—

"Whatever has been received, as a price, of workmen on houses, furniture and carriages, milking vessels and ornaments, is denominated a fee" (Śulka).‡

In the Vyavahâra-Mâdhavîya Mr. Burnell renders this verse as follows:—

"What is received as the price of utensils for the house, or cattle, or milch cows, for personal ornaments or for work, that is called *Śulka*." §

And Tagore, in the Vivâdachintâmańi:—

"The small sums which are received by a woman as the price or rewards of household duties, using household utensils, tending beasts of burden, looking after milch cattle, taking care of ornaments of dress, or superintending servants, are called her perquisites." ‖

The claims of a woman on the ground of Śulka would therefore be greatly different according to the rendering by Colebrooke, Burnell, or Tagore of the same authoritative passage.

An outcast, it is well known, is subject to legal disabilities; he is not allowed to testify, and he is excluded from inheritance. Now Sir W. Jones, and after him Tagore,¶ render the verse of Manu, IX., 202, in the following way:—

"But it is just that the heir who knows his duty should give all of

---

* IV., 1, 15. † P. 263. ‡ IV., 3, 19.
§ P. 41. ‖ P. 258. ¶ 'Vivâdach.,' p. 243.

them [viz. relatives who are excluded from inheritance] food and raiment for life without stint, according to the best of his power: he who gives them nothing *sinks assuredly to a region of punishment.*"

But in the *Mitâksharâ*,* where this passage from Manu is quoted, Colebrooke renders it:—

"But it is fit, that a wise man should give all of them food and raiment without stint to the best of his power: for he, who gives it not, shall be deemed *an outcast.*"

According to Sir W. Jones and Tagore, such a dereliction of duty would therefore entail a spiritual consequence only, but according to Colebrooke serious legal penalties too.

Without multiplying instances like these, I may now ask how could a judge, without a knowledge of Sanskrit, decide which of these scholars is right, or whether their difference of translation is based on a different reading of the same text, and if so, which of these different readings has a claim to greater authority than the rest? And if he cannot decide this question, what is to become of justice in all those cases that are governed by the law contained in these conflicting versions?

But as a Hindu has clearly a right to have justice done to him according to what are *his* real authorities, it is impossible to forego the question whether the present English translations of the law books can be implicitly relied upon as an equivalent for the originals.

On the whole, I have no doubt they may; and of all translations from Sanskrit into a European language I know of none to which, in my opinion, greater admiration is due than to the translation of Jîmûtavâhana's and Vijnâneśvara's law of inheritance by Colebrooke. So great, indeed, was the conscientiousness of that scholar, so thorough his understanding of the Hindu mind, and so vast and accurate his Sanskrit learning, that there is always the strongest reason for hesitation whenever one might feel disposed to question a rendering of his. And as Colebrooke's authority is still paramount in all law courts which have to deal with Hindu law, the aid afforded by his works to English judges cannot be too highly valued.

But, in the first place, the same high opinion cannot be entertained of all the translations already mentioned, for, with the exception of the version of the Vyavahâra-Mâdhavîya by Mr. Burnell, most of them are often too free and vague to be thoroughly reliable; and even the translation of the Vivâdachintâmaṅi by the late Prossonno C. Tagore, is

* II., 10, 5.

often more paraphrastic than is compatible with an accurate rendering of the text.

And in the second place, it should also be remembered that, apart from Burnell's, Tagore's, and Kristnasawmy's translations which appeared a few years ago, and those of Loiseleur Deslongchamps, Stenzler, and Roer, which may likewise be looked upon as relating to our own period, the remaining important works date from the end of the last and the earlier part of the present century, when there was not a single critical edition of any of their originals. Hence, with the MS. materials which have since come to light, with the numerous good editions of law texts to which it is now easy to refer,—I may here only name the admirable edition, by Bharatachandraśiromańi, of Jîmûtavâhana's Dâyabhâga, with seven commentaries, published under the patronage of P. C. Tagore, the various editions of Yâjñavalkya, with the whole Mitâksharâ, published at Calcutta, Benares, and Bombay, and several editions of Manu, with the commentary of Kullûkabhatta; in a word,—with the immense progress which Sanskrit studies have made for the last thirty years, both in India and Europe, it would be much more surprising if these translations were still found to stand the test of modern scholarship, than if they were found to fail.

And from this point of view alone must we judge of imperfections which occur, not only in Borradaile, Wynch, and Sutherland, but also in Sir W. Jones's translation of Manu, and even in Colebrooke's translations of the two treatises of Vijñâneśvara and Jîmûtavâhana. Yet that such imperfections exist, whatever the cause may be, is undeniable; and as even the accomplished work of Colebrooke is not entirely exempt from them, it may easily be inferred that they call for the attention of those who are answerable for the administration of the Hindu law.

To illustrate the nature of the imperfections of which I here speak, and which have a material bearing on the law of succession, I will choose some instances from Colebrooke's 'Two Treatises.'

In Jîmûtavâhana,* the right of the female line to succession is laid down in an important text from Vŕihaspati. According to Colebrooke this text runs thus:—

"The mother's sister, *the maternal uncle*, the father's sister, the mother-in-law, and the wife of an elder brother, are pronounced similar to mothers. If they leave no issue of their bodies, nor son [of a rival

* IV., 3, 31.

wife], nor daughter's son, nor son of those persons, the sister's son and the rest shall take their property."

That in a series of female relatives the "*maternal uncle*" should occur, and be declared to be similar to a mother, would in itself be improbable; nor is he really mentioned there; and the mistake seems to have been caused by an omission in the MS. used by Colebrooke; for according to the correct text the passage reads:—

"The mother's sister, *the wife of a maternal uncle, the paternal uncle's wife*, the father's sister, the mother-in-law, and the wife of an elder brother are pronounced similar to mothers. If they leave no issue of their body, nor son, nor daughter's son, nor son of those persons, the sister's son and the rest shall take their property."*

Hence the maternal uncle cannot claim on the ground of this passage, but in his stead the wife of a maternal uncle and the paternal uncle's wife can so claim.

In the same chapter, where the son's prior right to inheritance is mentioned,† a quotation from Vŕiddha-Śâtâtapa is made at the same time to show in what order the succession of other persons is regulated in accordance with the benefits which, through the Śrâddha rites, they may confer on the soul of the deceased. Colebrooke renders the passage as follows:—

"The son's preferable right too appears to rest on his presenting the greatest number of beneficial oblations, and on his rescuing his parent from hell. And a passage of Vŕiddha-Śâtâtapa expressly provides for the funeral oblations of *these women:* 'For the wife of a maternal uncle or of a sister's son, of a father-in-law and of a spiritual parent, of a friend and of a maternal grandfather, as well as for the sister of the mother or of the father, the oblation of food at obsequies must be performed. Such is the settled rule among those who are conversant with the Vedas.'"

The drift of the quotation from Vŕiddha-Śâtâtapa as it stands, would not be intelligible, for Jîmûtavâhana alleges his words, not in order to state *for* whom the Śrâddha should be performed, but *by whom* the benefits are conferred, and thus the title to inheritance in succession is acquired. But according to the words of the correct text, and the interpretation of them in the Dâyanirńaya, the passage from Vŕiddha-Śâtâtapa would have to be rendered thus:—

---

* Calc. 8vo ed., 1829 (p. 154); Bharatach.'s ed. (p. 172): mâtuḱ svasâ mâtulânî pitŕivyastrî pitŕisvasâ, śvaśrûḱ pûrvajapatnî cha mâtŕitulyâḱ prakîrtitâḱ; yadâsâm auraso na syât suto dauhitra eva vâ, tatsuto vâ dhanaḿ tâsâḿ svasrîyâdyâḱ samâpnuyuḱ.

† IV., 3, 36.

" . . . . And a passage of Vŕiddha-Śâtâtapa expressly provides for the funeral oblations of the following persons (*masc.*): the maternal uncle (performs the Śrâddha) for a sister's son, and a sister's son for his maternal uncle, (a son-in-law) for a father-in-law; (a pupil) for a spiritual teacher, (a friend) for a friend, and (a daughter's son) for a maternal grandfather. And also for the wives of these persons, and the sister of a mother and father, the oblation of food at obsequies must be performed. Such, &c."*

The importance of this passage had a recent illustration in the case of Gridhari Lall Roy *v.* the Government of Bengal. Gridhari was the maternal uncle of the father of a deceased Zemindar, whose inheritance he claimed, no other heirs claiming; but as the Bengal Government maintained that there was no law-text under which a maternal uncle could succeed to the property of a sister's son, it held that this was a case of escheat, and the High Court at Calcutta actually delivered a judgment in favour of the Crown. Now, since it has never been denied that a clear duty to perform the Śrâddha implies a right to succeed, there can be no doubt that the judgment of the High Court must have been different, had it been able to avail itself of the correct translation of the passage quoted, proving as that does, the maternal uncle's duty to perform the Śrâddha for a sister's son.

In Jîmûtavâhana,† according to Colebrooke, a grandmother and great grandmother would seem to have no right to succeed, inasmuch as they take no part in the Śrâddha. It is true that the passage alluded to would stand in direct contradiction with others in the same work, where the grandmother's and great grandmother's right is distinctly admitted, but

---

* The original passage, according to the text published in Calc. 1829 (p. 157), and Bharatach.'s edition (p. 175), is as follows:—Mâtulo bhâgineyasya svasrîyo mâtulasya cha, śvaśurasya guroś chaiva sakhyur mâtâmahasya cha, eteshâḿ chaiva bhâryâbhaḱ svasur mâtuḱ pitus tathâ, śrâddhadânaḿ tu kartavyam iti vedavidâḿ sthitir iti Vŕiddha-Śâtâtapa-vachanât. Amîshâḿ pińḋadatva-pratipâdanâd ayaḿ pińḋadânaviśeshâd adhikârakramaḱ.

In the *Dâyakaumudî*, where this passage from Śâtâtapa is quoted (ed. Calc., p. 155), the following comment from the *Dâyanirńaya* is appended to it: Mâtulo bhâgineyasya pińḋadaḱ; evaḿ svasrîyo mâtulasya pińḋadaḱ; śvaśurasya jâmâtâ pińḋadaḱ; guroḱ pińḋadâtâ śishyaḱ; mâtâmahasya pińḋadâtâ dauhitraḱ. Eteshâḿ mâtulâdînâḿ bhâryâbhyaḱ strîbhyaḱ śrâddhadânaḿ kartavyam iti vedârthopanibandhŕîṅâḿ nishṫhâ; iti Dâyanirńayaḱ.

† XI., 6, 3.

the fact is that no such contradiction results from the original text. Colebrooke's words are :—

"Nor can it be pretended that the stepmother, grandmother and great grandmother take their places at the funeral repast, in consequence of [ancestors being deified] with their wives."

Whereas the correct original text would in the translation run :—

"Nor can it be pretended that a stepmother, a stepmother of a father, and a stepmother of a paternal grandfather, take their places at the funeral repast, in consequence of [ancestors being deified] with their wives."*

In the translation of the Mitâksharâ †—for I will also add an instance or two from this treatise—a curious mistake has been caused by Colebrooke's adopting part of the translation by Sir W. Jones of a passage of Manu, quoted by Vijñâneśvara in support of his rule regarding effects not liable to partition.

"If the horses or the like," Vijñâneśvara says, "be numerous, they must be distributed among coheirs who live by the sale of them. If they cannot be divided, the number being unequal, they belong to the eldest brother, as ordained by Manu." And now follows the quotation from the latter,‡ which Colebrooke has rendered thus :—

"Let them never divide a single goat or sheep, or a single beast with uncloven hoofs : a single goat or sheep belongs to the first-born."

How, on the ground of such a text from Manu, the Mitâksharâ could forbid the division of an unequal number of cattle, would be unintelligible. But what Manu really says is :—

"If goats and sheep, together with beasts that have uncloven feet, are of an unequal number, let no division be made of them ; but let such an unequal number of goats and sheep (*v. l.* let such goat and sheep, with beasts that have uncloven feet,) go to the first-born."

The error arose from the translators mistaking the import of the singular number which is required by Sanskrit compounds to express collectiveness, and which in the case of the Dvandva compound *ajâvikam*

---

* Calc. ed. 1829 (p. 323), Bharatach.'s ed. (p. 332) : Na cha sapatnîkatvena sapatnîmâtuḱ sapatnîpitâmahyâḱ sapatnîprapitâmahyâś cha śrâddhe 'nupraveśaḱ. Compare the analogous passage in the *Vîramitrodaya*, f. 208, *b*, ll. 1 ff.

In this instance a printer's mistake perhaps caused the inaccuracy in Colebrooke's rendering ; for if we read in it "the step- mother, -grandmother," &c., the chief discrepancy would be removed.

† I., 4, 18. ‡ IX., 119.

"goats and sheep" is also interpreted in this sense by the commentator Kullûkabhatt́a, with a reference to the grammar of Pâńini.*

In the chapter which treats of the right of a widow to inherit the estate of one who leaves no male issue, the Mitâksharâ † says:—

"In the first place, the wife shares the estate. 'Wife' (patnî) signifies a woman espoused in lawful wedlock; conformably with the etymology of the term as implying a connexion with religious rites. *The singular number 'wife' (in the text of Yâjñavalkya) signifies the kind; hence if there are several wives belonging to the same or different castes, they divide the property according to the shares (prescribed to them), and take it.*"

The italicized words are entirely omitted in Colebrooke's translation, and as there is no other passage in the Mitâksharâ which relates to the emergency of several wives surviving a man who leaves no male issue, it is needless to point out how important they are in a disputed case of this nature. The omission, I may add, has already been noticed by Mr. Stokes in a note to page 53 of his 'Hindu Law Books,' where he comments on a passage of Borradaile's Vyavahâramayûkha.

I need not enlarge any further on mistakes of this nature, which, as I have already observed, may chiefly have arisen from the imperfect condition of MSS. which were used for the translations; but it is clear that they may become a serious impediment to rightful claims, and obstruct the course of justice.

Apart however from the question, whether a judge could entirely rely on these translations of Sanskrit law texts, it remains to be seen whether, even in their most perfect condition, the existing translations of the Hindu law books could be held to suffice for the settlement of the numerous cases that arise from disputes in matters of Hindu inheritance and adoption.

No one, I think, acquainted with the works enumerated at the commencement of this paper, and with other works of Sanskrit literature quoted by them, would affirm that they *do* suffice. He would, on the contrary, have to own that many law-books, as yet untranslated, are sometimes a material aid, and sometimes even indispensable, for a correct understanding of the Mitâksharâ and the digest of Jîmûtavâhana.

The *Vîramitrodaya*, for instance, is to a large extent a full commentary on the Mitâksharâ, which it copiously quotes; and the same may be

* *Mit.* (I., 4, 18): Ajâvikań saikaśaphań na jâtu vishamań bhajet, ajâvikań tu vishamań (*v. l.* saikaśaphań) jyesht́hasyaiva vidhîyate, iti Manu-smarańât.—*Kullûkabhatt́a* to *Manu*, IX., 119: ajâvikam iti paśudvandvâd vibhâshayaikavadbhâvah́ (comp. Pâń. II., 4, 11).

† II., 1, 5.

said of the *Smṛitichandrikâ*, of which a few years ago not a line had appeared in print, and of which even now a trustworthy translation cannot be said to exist. Again, the seven commentaries on Jîmûtavâhana's Dâyabhâga, Raghunandana's Smṛititattva, the treatises of Kamalâkara, the Dâyakaumudî, and kindred works, are in numerous instances the best, if not the only, means for arriving at the precise meaning of its text. And so long as all these works remain untranslated, justice to the Hindus in matters of inheritance must remain uncertain, because it would often have to depend on the reasoning of the European mind, which, failing to appreciate the historical facts and the religious ground on which Hindu reasoning proceeds, must necessarily often become fallacious. In a recent case tried in the High Court at Fort William, the Chief Justice gave the advice, not to introduce English notions into cases governed by Hindu law. "The Hindu law of inheritance," he very justly observed, "is based upon the Hindu religion, and we must be cautious that in administering Hindu law we do not, by acting upon our notions derived from English law, inadvertently wound or offend the religious feelings of those who may be affected by our decisions; or lay down principles at variance with the religions of those whose law we are administering."—(In the High Court of Judicature at Fort William. Ordinary original civil jurisdiction, 1st September, 1869. Gannendro Mohun Tagore *v.* Opendro Mohun Tagore, &c., p. 23.)

Yet how much even judges of the highest standing are liable to err, if, for a knowledge of the positive Hindu law, they substitute that which from an English point of view may appear to be the most logical and faultless reasoning, will be seen by the instance of a Privy Council judgment which, if relied upon as a precedent, would materially alter the whole Hindu law of inheritance in one of its vital points.

The judgment I am here alluding to is that delivered on the 30th of November, 1863, by the Judicial Committee of the Privy Council upon the appeal of Kattama Nauchear *v.* the Râjâ of Śivaganga, from the Sudder Devanny Adawlut at Madras.

The object of the litigation was the Zemindary of Śivaganga, situated in the Madras Presidency. Its last owner, who was in undisputed possession of it, had died in 1829, leaving no male issue, but several wives by whom he had daughters; and the daughter of one of those wives was the appellant in the case; for the Sudder Court at Madras had decided against her claims, and pronounced in favour of the respondent, a nephew of the deceased, who at the time of the appeal was in possession of the Zemindary.

The issues of the case, as stated in the judgment of the Judicial Committee of the Privy Council, were these :—

1. Were Gaurivallabha (the deceased Râjâ) and his brother (for the grandson of the latter was the respondent, the Râjâ in possession) undivided in estate, or had a partition taken place between them?

2. If they were undivided, was the Zemindary the self-acquired and separate property of Gaurivallabha (the deceased Râjâ)? And if so—

3. What is the course of succession according to the Hindu law of the south of India of such an acquisition, where the family is in other respects an undivided family?

The first of these questions the judgment of the Judicial Committee of the Privy Council answered in the sense that the deceased Râjâ and his brother were *undivided* in estate; and this being a question of fact, we have simply to accept their Lordships' finding.

In regard to the second question, the judgment held that the Zemindary was not the ancestral, but the self-acquired and separate property of the late Râjâ; and this, too, being a question of fact, no remark has to be added to it.

Concerning the third, however, which is a question of law, the judgment went on to say, that according to the law in the south of India, as affecting members of an undivided family, the Zemindary would have passed to the nephew had it been ancestral property, but being self-acquired property, the daughter of one of the widows—the appellant in the case—was entitled to it.

Now, in the first place, I must here observe that this judgment is exclusively based on what their Lordships consider to be the law of the Mitâksharâ. That the Mitâksharâ is *one* of the law authorities in the south of India is unquestionable; but it is likewise an undisputed fact that it is not the *primary* authority in that part of India. As before stated, the Mitâksharâ, which is merely a running commentary on the text of Yâjñavalkya, is incomplete in many respects; and amongst the later works which enlarged on it and supplied its defects, the digests called *Smṛitichandrikâ* and *Vyavahâra-Mâdhavîya* became the chief authorities in the south. At the time when the Śivaganga case was pending, Mr. Burnell's translation of the Mâdhavîya did not exist, nor even the imperfect version of the Smṛitichandrikâ by Mr. Kristnasawmy Iyer. These works were then accessible only as Sanskrit MSS. Hence not so much as an allusion to them occurs in the judgment of the Judicial Committee of the Privy Council; and while it is not denied that the respondent had a right to have his claims dealt with according to the recognized *primary* law of his country, we here meet with the anomalous circumstance that they were decided upon according to what in the south of India is only considered as a secondary source of law.

And that this distinction is not merely a fortuitous one is proved by the case itself. For there is no text in the Mitâksharâ which clearly provides for it, whereas there are passages in the *Smṛitichandrikâ* and the *Mâdhavîya* which, I have no doubt, would have proved to their Lordships' minds that the second question they had raised was irrelevant to the case, and that their final decision was even contrary to the very spirit of the law of the Mitâksharâ.

But as they were not acquainted with the two Digests which, while in perfect accordance with the Mitâksharâ, elucidate its obscurities, their Lordships supplied the apparent defect of the Mitâksharâ with arguments which, from a European point of reasoning, might bear out the conclusion at which they arrived, but from a Hindu point of view do not.

I have already mentioned that the family of the appellant and the respondent were admittedly undivided in estate. Yet in a family of *this* description the judgment of the Judicial Committee raised the question as to what was in it ancestral, and what was self-acquired, property. Such a question, however, cannot judicially occur in an *undivided* family, so long as it remains undivided, which was here the case. The translated text of the Mitâksharâ itself is silent on the law of succession in reference to an undivided family, for the text of Yâjñavalkya, which this commentary follows verse by verse, does not deal with it; and in the first section of its second chapter, which treats of the right of widows to inherit in default of male issue, and on which the judgment in this case is exclusively based, nothing is stated affecting the rights of any member of an undivided family. On the other hand, the *Vyavahâra-Mâdhavîya*, and especially the *Smṛitichandrikâ*, very distinctly regulate the succession rights in an undivided family: it results from them that only a male member of such a family can be heir, and that *so long as the family remains undivided*, the whole of the property, whether ancestral or self-acquired, is vested in him.* The reasons of such a law are likewise clear. In an undivided family the principal religious duties are undivided, and the benefits, therefore, to be bestowed on the soul of the deceased ancestor—benefits on which the right of succession rests—can be conferred only by one single member of the family, its actual head.†

Not having before them this distinct law, which is quite in harmony

---

* The question, therefore, what is ancestral and what is self-acquired property, can judicially only occur at the time when division takes place.

† See Appendix.

with the law of Manu and all other legislators, and being left in doubt by a section of the Mitâksharâ, which having nothing whatever to do with the case in question could of course not enlighten them, the Lords of the Judicial Committee laid down a perfectly novel proposition which, if adopted, would alter the basis of the whole Hindu law.

"There are two principles," the judgment says,* "on which the rule of succession, according to the Hindu law, appears to depend: the first is that which determines the right to offer the funeral oblation, and the degree in which the person making the offering is supposed to minister to the spiritual benefit of the deceased; the other is an assumed right of survivorship."

But the fact is, that there is only *one* principle, that stated by the Report in the first proposition, and that the second does not exist at all. Of the first, Sir W. Jones had already said that it contains the key to the *whole* Hindu law of inheritance; and even the single text which the judgment adduces in support of its theory of a right of survivorship, had it been quoted in full, and with the remarks attached to it by the Smŕitichandrikâ, would have shown that no such right can be inferred from it.†

---

* Page 18.

† After the words above quoted ("there are two principles . . . . . right of survivorship") the Report continues:—"Most of the authorities rest the uncontested right of widows to inherit the estates of their husbands, dying separated from their kindred, on the first of these principles (1 Strange, 135). But some ancient authorities also invoke the other principle (viz. that of survivorship). Vŕihaspati (3 Dig. 458, tit. cccxcix; see also Sir W. Jones' paper cited 2 Strange, 250) says:—'Of him whose wife is not deceased half the body survives; how should another take the property, while half the body of the owner lives?'" The text here quoted by the judgment reads, however, in full, as quoted by the Smŕitichandrikâ, thus:—"In Scripture, in the traditional code, and in popular practice, a wife (*patnî*) is declared by the wise to be half the body (of her husband), *equally sharing the fruit of* (*his*) *pure and impure acts* (*i. e.* of virtue and vice). Of him whose wife is not deceased, half the body lives; how then should another take his property while half the body of the owner lives? Although Sakulyas (distant kinsmen), although his father, his mother, and uterine brothers be present, the wife of him who died, leaving no male issue, shall take his share." (The same passage also occurs in Jîmûtavâhana's Dâyabhâga, XI., 1, 2, and in Sir W. Jones' paper, 2 Strange, 250, mentioned by the Report.) The Smŕitichandrikâ (Calc. ed., p. 58) *introduces* this passage with the following words:—"Accordingly, after having pronounced that compared to other (relatives) a wife has a nearer claim *on account of the circumstance that she has the property of conferring visible and spiritual benefits* (on the deceased),

The judgment further asks:—"If the first of these principles (the spiritual principle) were the only one involved, it would not be easy to see why the widow's right of inheritance should not extend to her husband's share in an undivided estate."

This question is perfectly pertinent, but it is one of the great points of difference between the Dâyabhâga- and the Mitâksharâ schools. The former assuming that under any conditions the widow would confer the greatest spiritual benefits on the soul of a deceased husband, provided he leaves no male issue, in consequence rules that, in such an emergency, she is *always* entitled to succeed to the property of the husband, whether the latter be divided or not. The Mitâksharâ school, on the contrary, not admitting this superior spiritual power of a widow in an *undivided family*, excludes her from the position she holds in the Dâyabhâga school. But the Śivaganga case fell under the law of the Mitâksharâ school, and it is not for *us* to decide whether the view of the latter regarding the *spiritual* power of a wife is, or is not, more correct than that of the Dâyabhâga school.

In short, "there being no positive text governing the case before the Judicial Committee"*—simply because their Lordships could not refer to the very law authorities conformably to which alone the case should have been decided—they relied on an irrelevant text of the Mitâksharâ, and in applying the law of succession which is applicable only to a divided family, to an undivided one, even mistook this text itself.

That this judgment, if accepted as an authoritative interpretation of the Hindu law, would introduce a second principle, hitherto unknown, into the Hindu right of inheritance, and would entirely alter this law so far as undivided Hindu families are concerned, requires no further re-

---

Vṛihaspati has shown that the wife has the share of her husband's property, if there are no secondary (or adopted) sons, though father and other heirs as far downwards as the Sakulyas may be alive." Again, after having explained the import of the word "wife (*patní*)" in the passage quoted, the same law authority says:—"Accordingly, the term *patní* gives us to understand that *her fitness to perform such religious acts, as the rites in honour of the manes, is the reason that she is entitled to take the share of her husband.*" It is clear, therefore, that though "acting upon our notions derived from English law," we might feel induced to infer from the word "lives," in the alleged passage, a right of survivorship, the Hindu mind, and especially the very law authority on which the judgment should have been based, was far from following such a course of reasoning. It looked, on the contrary, upon this passage as confirming the *spiritual* principle, and this principle alone.

* Page 16.

mark. But it seems equally clear that such a result could never have occurred if the Lords of the Judicial Committee had been in possession of more law texts than at the time were accessible to them.

Another instance of the insufficiency of the law texts as hitherto translated, is afforded by the judgment of the High Court of Calcutta in the matter Gridhari Lall Roy *v.* the Government of Bengal, to which I have already had occasion to refer. And as it implies a large class of cases which may equally suffer from the same cause, it will not be deemed superfluous to draw attention to it.

I have just pointed out the great principle on which the Hindu law of inheritance is based. A kind of spiritual bargain is at the root of it. For the *direct* or *indirect* benefit of his future life, a person requires after his death certain religious ceremonies—the Śrâddha—to be performed for him; and since these ceremonies entail expense, his property is supposed to be the equivalent for such expense. A *direct* benefit from the Śrâddha is derived, for instance, by a father, grandfather, and great-grandfather, to whom the funeral cakes are offered by a son, grandson, or great-grandson; and an indirect benefit, by a deceased whose relatives present the funeral cakes to his *maternal*, grandfather, great-grandfather, and great-great-grandfather; for by doing so, they perform for him that duty which, when alive, he would have been bound to perform.* Since, however, the nearer a person is related to the deceased, the greater is the direct or indirect benefit which he is able to confer on the latter's soul, the nearer, too, are his claims to the inheritance. But in the same degree as a person owes the Śrâddha to a relative, the purity of his body is also affected by the death of that relative; and the time within which the impurity he suffers in consequence can be removed by certain religious acts, depends therefore on the degree of relationship in which he stood to the deceased. Again, the right of marriage is affected by the degree of relationship, for within certain degrees marriage is strictly forbidden by the Hindu law.

To obtain, therefore, an authoritative explanation of what, to a Hindu, are the degrees of relationship—and on these degrees, again, depends the *order* of succession—we have especially to look to those portions of the codes of law, and those separate treatises, which relate to the performance of the Śrâddha, to the laws concerning impurity and the removal of it, and to the laws of marriage. All that occurs in regard to these important topics under the head of inheritance is but incidentally stated

---

* See *e. g. Jîmûtavâhana*, XI., 1, 34; XI., 6, 13.

there, as serving the argument in point, but not with a view of being an exhaustive treatment of the matter. On the whole, there is but little to be gathered from the chapter of inheritance regarding the *relative* rights of heirs; and if the number of such heirs is large, and the degrees of their affinity are intricate, there would be a considerable difficulty in deducing from the general argument merely, the precise right of a particular heir.

Now, in a complete code of law like that of Manu or Yâjñavalkya the subject of Śrâddha, impurity and marriage, is dealt with in the *âchâra* and *prâyaśchitta* (the first and third) portions of the work, not in the second, a portion of which is devoted to inheritance. But as of the commentatorial works on Manu, of the whole Mitâksharâ on the first and third books of Yâjñavalkya, of the great work of Raghunandana, and of the numerous important works and treatises dealing with these topics, such as the Nirṅayasindhu, Dharmasindhusâra, Śrâddhaviveka, Śrâddhanirṅaya, Âchâradarśa, and many others, nothing whatever as yet exists in translation, it may easily be surmised that judges unable to read these works in the original language are deprived of a very important means of deciding on the relative rights of claimants to successions, and that in many instances their decisions may be at fault; for I do not think that, without a positive knowledge of the Hindu religion in its greatest detail, any European could undertake to say whether, for instance, a brother confers more or less benefit on the soul of a brother than his daughter's son; or whether a maternal grandmother on the father's side enjoys that privilege in a higher or lower degree than a paternal grandmother on the mother's side. In the judgment of the High Court at Calcutta, on the case to which I am about to attach some remarks, the learned judges indeed say: "It would be difficult for a person at the present day to give a clear and intelligible reason for many of the eccentricities and anomalies which characterize Hindu law of all schools, and this notwithstanding the encomium of the Pleader on its stern logic and uncompromising adherence to principles once laid down." * But what in this passage is called "eccentricities and anomalies," is nothing but the consequence of the religious views on which the Śrâddha ceremonies rest. It is certainly difficult—nay, impossible—to understand this consequence without a knowledge of its cause, but the latter once mastered in its detail, I believe that "the encomium of the Pleader" would not be found an exaggerated one.

* Gridhari Lall Roy *v.* the Bengal Government. 'Record,' p. 98.

The case in question is the one already alluded to,* and the judgment which the High Court at Calcutta passed on it is highly instructive in several respects, for it tells us that a maternal uncle is to a Hindu no heir at all, even if no other relatives of the deceased dispute his claim. To understand this extraordinary finding, it is necessary to see from what premises it was deduced.

According to the degrees of relationship, the old lawgivers divided heirs into three categories, the first being that of the *Sapiṅḍas*, or kindred connected by the *Piṅḍa* or the funeral cake offered at the Śrâddha, and extending to the seventh degree (including the survivor) in the ascending and descending male line; the second, consisting of the *Samânodakas*, or kindred connected by the libation of (udaka) water only offered at the Śrâddha, who extend to the fourteenth degree; and the third, comprising the so-called *Bandhus* or *Bândhavas*, who, in the chapter of the Mitâkshara and the Dâyabhâga treating of them, Colebrooke generally renders *cognates*. It was as one of the last category that Gridhari claimed as the maternal uncle of the father of a deceased Zemindar. But the judges of the High Court of Bengal did not allow the claim, on the ground that he was excluded from the right of inheritance by the definition given of the term *bandhu*, in the sixth section of the second chapter of the Mitâksharâ. The passage on which the judgment relied runs thus:—

"*Bandhus* (cognates) are of three kinds; related to the person himself, to his father, or to his mother: as is declared by the following text. 'The sons of his own father's sister, the sons of his own mother's sister, and the sons of his own maternal uncle, must be considered as *his own Bandhus.* The sons of his father's paternal aunt, the sons of his father's maternal aunt, and the sons of his father's maternal uncle, must be deemed *his father's Bandhus.* The sons of his mother's paternal aunt, the sons of his mother's maternal aunt, and the sons of his mother's maternal uncle, must be reckoned *his mother's Bandhus.*'"†

Now, as in this list the *sons* of a father's maternal uncle are called *Bandhu*, but not the father's maternal uncle himself, and as Gridhari did not pretend that he was either a *Sapiṅḍa* or a *Samânodaka*, he was nowhere.

His plea was, that the enumeration contained in the quoted text was *not an exhaustive one*, but merely an illustration of the line in which relatives called *Bandhu* must be sought for; that a father's maternal uncle stood in the same position to *his* son (named in that list) as a maternal uncle to *his* (also named there); and since a maternal uncle, he argued,

* P. 13.

† Two Treatises, &c., p. 352.

was clearly intended to be included in the list, a father's maternal uncle belonged to the relatives of the Bandhu category. The correctness of the analogy was admitted by the judgment,* but it still denied that a maternal uncle *was* intended to be included in the list. The Lords of the Judicial Committee of the Privy Council, admitting the appellant's plea, reinstated him in his right, and there can be no question that they did justice to his claim; but as the arguments on which their judgment was based would have been stronger, and would have been less hypothetical, than they now are, had their Lordships been able to avail themselves of more and of safer texts than were at their disposal, and as neither the Bengal Government could ever have claimed the inheritance of Woopendro, nor the High Court of Calcutta pronounced against the Bandhu quality of a "maternal uncle," had they possessed the same advantage, it falls within the scope of this paper to illustrate by this case the serious deficiencies which in the present administration of the Hindu law must be unavoidable.

There were several ways of ascertaining whether the list of Bandhus relied upon by the Bengal Government, was an exhaustive one or not; or in other words, whether a father's maternal uncle and a maternal uncle were included in, or excluded from, it.

The first was to consult any of the works authoritatively treating of the duty of persons to perform the Śrâddha, or of impurity which would affect relatives in consequence of a death, for as all such persons are eventually heirs, it would have been seen at once whether the few individuals named in the quoted text could possibly have been intended for an *exhaustive* definition of the Bandhu category. Now, in all such works, *e. g.* the Dharmasindhusâra, the Nirńayasindhu, Raghunandana's Śuddhitattva, &c., this category comprises all the connections on the mother's side up to the seventh degree in the ascending and descending line; and I may almost say, as a matter of course, the maternal uncle is distinctly mentioned by them. Even the passage from Jîmûtavâhana's Dâyabhâga, adduced above,† might of itself have proved that in the absence of nearer relatives the "maternal uncle" has the right of performing the funeral rites for a sister's son, and it would have confirmed a similar conclusion resulting from the same Digest,‡ for in regard to a question like this there is no difference between the various schools. The judgment of the Judicial Committee says: §—"Mr. Forsyth, indeed, argued strongly against the right of the appellant to inherit, on the assumption that he was

* Record, p. 96, line 62.

† P. 13.

‡ XI., 6, 12 and 13.

§ P. 3.

not entitled to offer the funeral oblations. But is this assumption well founded? There is evidence, the uncontradicted evidence of the family priest and others, that the appellant did, in point of fact, perform the shradh of Woopendro; and he seems, in the judgment of the priest, properly to have performed that function in the absence of any nearer kinsman." But the judgment adds:—"It is, however, unnecessary to determine whether this act of the appellant was regular or not. The issue in this case is not between two competing kinsmen, but between a kinsman of the deceased and the Crown." Yet on the *regularity* of this act all really depends, since the right of performing the Śrâddha and that of succeeding are convertible terms, and, in the extreme case of an escheat to the Crown, even the king inherits only on the condition that he provides for the funeral rites of the person to whom he succeeds, and the king is debarred from succession to a Brâhman's property, because a man of the second or an inferior caste cannot minister to the soul of one of the first. That the family priest allowed the appellant to perform the Śrâddha for his nephew, certainly raised a strong presumption in favour of the maternal uncle's right to do so; but the *certainty* whether he really possessed this right could be established only on the ground of authoritative texts.

The second mode of settling the doubt consisted in referring to the decision of other authorities of the Mitâksharâ school; and of these, it would have been found that, for instance, the *Vivâdachintâmaṅi*, after quoting the same passage describing the three categories of Bandhus, as the Mitâksharâ, sums up its discussion by giving a list of heirs, amongst whom "the *maternal uncle and the rest*" correspond with the Bandhus of the Mitâksharâ.* The Lords of the Judicial Committee had the advantage of being able to resort to this method, since an important passage from the *Vîramitrodaya*—a digest which, as already observed, is often a full commentary on the Mitâksharâ—was accessible to them in a translation given at p. 15 of the Record; and they very justly referred to it in order to show that this authority included "the maternal uncle" in the Bandhu list alleged by the Mitâksharâ. But it so happened that they had ground to suspect the correctness of the translation of this passage in one particular, and in consequence amended it hypothetically where it appeared to them to be at fault. Their conjecture was perfectly right; but as this was the only passage of the kind from works of the Mitâksharâ school, on which they had to rely for *this* argument, it would doubtless

---

* See Tagore, pp. 298, 299; Sanskrit text, Calc. 1837, pp. 155, 156: . . . . vyavahitasakulyas tadabhâve mâtulâdiḥ.

have been much more satisfactory had they been in possession of an authoritative translation of the work to which the passage belongs.*

The third and most accurate course of all was to ascertain whether the author of the Mitâksharâ himself, by whose law the case was governed, elsewhere gave a definition of the term used by him, since, according to the first principle of interpretation, such a definition would necessarily remove all doubts. That the Lords of the Judicial Committee and the learned judges below endeavoured to adopt this course also, it is needless to say; but for the reasons already explained, the materials at their disposal did not enable them to arrive at anything like a safe conclusion.

One obstacle that lay in their way arose from the fact, that Colebrooke in his 'Two Treatises' had accidentally varied the translation of the term Bandhu, and therefore made its identification in several places impossible. Thus in the *Mitâksharâ*, II., 1, 2; 5, 3; 6, 1 and 2, and in *Jîmûtavâhana*, XI., 1, 4; and 6, 12, he had rendered *bandhu* 'cognate,' or 'cognate kindred'; but in *Mitâksharâ*, II., 7, 1, 'relations'; in II., 12, 1 and 2, 'relatives'; in II., 11, 6, 'kindred,' and 'relations'; and in *Jîmûtavâhana*, XI., 1, 5, 'kinsmen.' Had he not done so, the learned

* The judgment says (p. 7):—"After stating that the term 'Sakulya' or distant kinsman found in the text of Manu, comprehends the three kinds of cognates, the commentator goes on to say,—'The term cognates (*Bandhus*) in the text of Jogishwara must comprehend also the maternal uncles and the rest, otherwise the maternal uncles and the rest would be omitted, and their sons would be entitled to inherit, and not they themselves, though nearer in the degree of affinity, a doctrine highly objectionable.' The passage as translated at p. 15 of the Record has '*then* they themselves,' in place of '*not* they themselves.' If this be the correct reading, it would follow that even if the exclusion of the maternal uncle and others not mentioned in the text relied upon by the respondents from the list of Bandhus were established, they would still, as relations, be heirs, whose title would be preferable to that of the king." But oddly enough, at p. 24 of the Record where a translation of the same passage from the Vîramitrodaya occurs, the last words read: "and *then* they themselves, though *never* in the degree of affinity. A doctrine highly objectionable. Quoted from the Beermithodoya." According to the Sanskrit text of the Vîramitrodaya (Calc. 1815, p. 209, *b*. l. 8) there can be no doubt that "not they themselves" is the correct rendering; and that "*never*" is probably a misprint for "*nearer*"; yet as it is a common occurrence in the Indian courts that Pandits consulted by the litigants differ in their rendering of the same text (compare also the note to p. 28) how is a judge, not knowing Sanskrit, to decide which rendering is legitimate?

judges at Calcutta and the Lords of the Judicial Committee would have found that in its commentary on the verse where Yâjñavalkya says that "in a case of disputed partition the truth should be ascertained by the evidence of relatives called *jñâti*, relatives called *bandhu*, by (other) witnesses, written proof or separate possession of house or field," the Mitâksharâ * explains relatives called jñâti, "bandhus on the father's side"; relatives called *bandhu*, "bandhus on the mother's side, viz. the maternal uncle and the rest."† And this definition of *bandhu* is sub-

---

* II., 12, 2.

† *Yâjñ.*, II., 150: vibhâganihnave jñâtibandhusâkshyabhilekhitaih́, vibhâgabhâvanâ jñeyâ gŕihakshetraiś cha yautukaih́; whereupon the *Mit.* in both *Calcutta* editions (1815 and 1829) remarks: vibhâgasya nihnave 'palâpe, jñâtibhih́ pitŕibandhubhih́ sâkshibhir mâtulâdibhir mâtŕibandhubhih́ pûrvoktalakshańaih́, &c.; in the *Benares* ed. (1853), vibhâgasya nihnave 'palâpe, jñâtibhih́ pitŕibandubhir mâtulâdibhih́ sâkshibhih́ pûrvoktalakshańaih́, &c.; in the *Bombay* ed. (1863), vibhâgasya nihnave 'palâpe jñâtibhih́ pitŕibandubhir mâtŕibandhubhir mâtulâdibhih́ sâkshibhih́ pûrvoktalakshanaih́, &c. In the *Benares* edition the word *mâtŕibandhubhih́* is evidently by mistake omitted before mâtulâdibhih́; and in the *Bombay* edition the order of the text-words of Yâjñav., *jñâti*, *bandhu*, *sâkshin*, is more closely followed than in the Calcutta editions, where the order is *jñâti*, *sâkshin*, *bandhu*. But unless in the latter editions this inversion is the printer's mistake only—which is very possible on account of the severing of sâkshibhih́ and pûrvoktalakshańaih́—it may have been intended to show that *pitŕibandhubhih́* is the explanation of *jñâtibhih́*, and *mâtulâdibhih́*, *mâtŕibandhubhih́*, that of *bandhubhih́*, whereas otherwise it might be supposed (as Colebrooke did), that *jñâtibhih́* had been left unexplained, and pitŕibandhubhir mâtulâdibhir mâtŕibandhubhih́ were the words explaining *bandhubhih́*. That the former view, however, is the correct one, results from the following parallel passages in which the text of Yâjñ. is commented upon: *Vîramitrodaya* (p. 223 *a*, l. 4, 5), vibhâgasya nihnave 'palâpe vibhaktamadhye kenachit kŕite jñâtibhih́ pitŕibandhubhih́, bandhubhir mâtulâdibhih́, sâkshibhih́, &c.; *Vyavahâra-Mâdhavîya* (MSS.), jñâtayah́ pitŕibândhavâh́, bândhavâs tu mâtulâdayah́ (*v. l.* mâtŕibândhavâś cha; or without *cha*); *Jîmûtavâhana* (p. 359), prathamaḿ jñâtayah́ sapińd́âh́ sâkshińah́, tadabhâve bandhupadopanîtâh́ sambandhinah́, tadabhâva udâsînâ api sâkshińah́ (comp. 'Two Treatises,' p. 237; ch. xiv., § 3). Hence Colebrooke's rendering of Mit., II., 12, § 2, "if partition be denied or disputed, the fact may be known and certainty be obtained by the testimony of kinsmen, relatives of the father or of the mother, such as maternal uncles and the rest, being competent witnesses as before described"—has to be altered into: "if partition be denied or disputed, the fact may be known and certainty be obtained by (the testimony of) relatives called *jñâti*, viz. the bandhus on the father's side; or (that of) relatives called *bandhu*, viz. the bandhus on the mother's side, such as maternal uncles and the rest, or (other) witnesses, as before described."

stantially therefore the same as that given by the Mitâksharâ,* where it defines *bandhu* as "a Sapińda of a different family,"† that is, a Sapińda on the mother's side. Nor does Jîmûtavâhana differ on this point from the Mitâksharâ school, for when speaking of the sense in which Yâjña-valkya understood the word *bandhu*, he says,‡ "to intimate that the *maternal uncle* shall inherit in consequence of the proximity of oblations, as presenting offerings to the maternal grandfather and the rest, which the deceased was bound to offer, Yâjñavalkya employs the term *bandhu*."

But there are other passages, also, in the Mitâksharâ which clearly show that its author did not intend to quote the list of the three categories of Bandhus as an exhaustive one. They are contained, however, in that portion of the Mitâksharâ not translated by Colebrooke. One of these had been supplied to the High Court at Calcutta for the purposes of the suit, but was singularly misunderstood by it. In Book II., v. 264, Yâjñavalkya where speaking of co-traders lays down this rule; "if one (of them) having gone to a foreign country, dies, let the heirs, the *bândhavas*, *jñâtis*, or those who have come, take the property; and in their default the king." Whereupon the Mitâksharâ comments: "When of partners 'one who has gone to a foreign country dies,' then let 'the heirs,' that is, his son or other lineal descendants; 'the *bândhavas*,' that is, *the relatives on the mother's side*, viz. *the maternal uncle and the rest*; 'the *jñâtis*,' that is Sapińdas, except the lineal descendants; 'or those who have come,' that is, the partners in business who have come from the foreign country, take his share; and 'in their default,' that is, in default of 'the heirs,' &c., let the king take it."§

---

* II., 5, 3.

† Bhinnagotrâńâm sapińdânâm bandhuśabdena grahańât.

‡ XI., 6, 12.

§ The translation of this passage as given by me above differs from that which the Bengal Government had laid before the High Court, and it also differs from that tendered by the Appellant to the Court. The Record (p. 97) says:

"The words are, as translated by the Defendant, Respondent [*i. e.* the Bengal Government]:—

"*Text.*—'When one dies in a foreign country, let the descendants (Bundhoos), cognates, gentiles, or his companions, take the goods, or, in their default, the king.'

"*Commentary.*—'When he who is gone to a foreign country, of those who are associated in trade, dies, then his share should be inherited by his heirs, *i. e.* the son and other descendants, *viz.*, (Bundhoos) cognates, *i. e.*, those on the mother's side, the maternal uncle, and others, *viz.*, the gentiles, *i. e.*, the Sapindahs, besides the son and other descendants, and

In this passage the High Court at Calcutta declared "The words, maternal uncle and the rest," to be "an insertion over and above what is contained in the principal text as to Bundhoos"; and added: "Under these circumstances, as the translated passage refers to an exceptional state of things, it may be that the ordinary succession has been interfered with in a particular other than that above suggested, though the succession professes to follow the ordinary course in all other particulars save one."*

It need scarcely be observed that there is not the slightest ground

---

those who are come, *i. e.*, those among them associated in trade, from a foreign country, or in their default, the king shall take.' "

No wonder that the Appellant objected to this jumble of words, where in the '*Text*,' 'Bundhoos' would be an explanation of 'descendants,' instead of 'cognates'; and in the *Commentary*, too, 'Bundhoos' and 'gentiles' are made to explain the same word 'descendants'; and the word 'besides' is intended for '*except*.' But neither is the Appellant's version unobjectionable. It is given after the foregoing quotation, by the Record, in these words:

"*Text.*—A person having gone to a foreign country, his goods would be taken by his heir, and those related *through a Bundhoo, or to a Bundhoo* or agnatic relation, or person returning from that country. In default of heirs, the king will take." And his translation of the Commentary of the Mitâksharâ is as follows:

"When a person from amongst the persons trading in fellowship, or common stock, goes to a foreign country and dies there, his share will be taken by his heir, *i. e.* offspring, *i. e.* son and other offspring, Bundhoos, relations on the mother's side, maternal uncles, and the rest, or others, agnatic relations, that is to say, Sapindas, other than offspring, or by those coming back. Those who amongst the co-traders return from a foreign country, shall take; in default of them, the king."

If this version were correct (I am not here alluding to the last sentence which is perhaps misprinted for ". . . . coming back; *viz.* those who . . . ."), the *text* of Yâjñavalkya would treat of persons who are "related *through a Bandhu*, or *to a Bandhu*," while the *commentary* of the Mitâksharâ would speak of Bandhus only; and as the words "related through a Bandhu, or to a Bandhu" are meant for Yâjñavalkya's word *bândhava*, it would follow that relatives called *bândhava* are more distant heirs than those called *bandhu*. Nor should I feel surprised if possibly a doubt of this kind had some influence on the High Court, when, as we shall see, it founded a very strange theory on this passage. But *bândhava*, though a derivative of *bandhu*, has absolutely the same sense as the latter, as results, not only from all the law-commentaries, but also from the grammatical Gaṅa prajñâdi to *Pâṅini* V. 4, 38.—Here then are two litigants, both differently rendering the same important text to which they appeal; and a Law Court, unable to examine this text in the original, is to decide which of them is right, or whether both are wrong!

* Record, p. 98.

for such a theory; and the judgment of the Judicial Committee of the Privy Council very justly remarks (p. 7): "Their Lordships cannot admit the reasonableness of this hypothesis, and think that even on the Mitâksharâ the question under consideration is at least uncertain." Yet instead of affording *absolute* proof that the definition here given by the Mitâksharâ of the term *bândhava* or *bandhu* is in accordance with the definition which the same work *everywhere* gives when it thinks proper to paraphrase the word *bandhu*, and that consequently no new definition was here intended for an "exceptional state of things," the judgment of the Judicial Committee proceeds to fortify its position by the passage, above alleged, from the Vîramitrodaya, and therefore does *not* remove the doubt whether the Mitâksharâ itself countenanced the theory objected to or not.

Yet one such definition of *bandhu*, literally agreeing with that in the passage just quoted, might have been found in the passage mentioned before;* and another, occurring in another, untranslated portion of the Mitâksharâ, is still more explicit; for it distinctly refers to the very passage in question, which contains the Bandhu list, and settles therefore even the last remnant of uncertainty.

In Book III., v. 24, Yâjñavalkya, treating of the season of impurity caused by the death of friends, says: "Purification lasts a day when a guru dies, or a boarder, a vedic teacher, a *maternal uncle* or a Brâhman versed in one vedic school." On which words the Mitâksharâ remarks: "'Guru' means a spiritual teacher; 'boarder,' a pupil; 'vedic teacher,' him who explains the Vedângas. By the word '*maternal uncle*,' the relatives on the female side, viz. the bandhus of one's self, the mother's bandhus, and the father's bandhus are implied; and who these are has been shown in (the commentary on) the verse of Yâjñavalkya, which begins with the words, 'the wife and the daughters,'" † that is, on the very same verse, II., 135 (Coleb., p. 324), to which the whole commentary of Sects. 1-7 of ch. ii. of the Mitâksharâ, and consequently also that of Sect. 6 (Coleb., p. 352) belongs.

In short, the maternal uncle, so far from being *excluded* from the *Bandhus*, is almost invariably named as the very type of the whole category; and what relative indeed on the mother's side could have a nearer claim to that title than he?

Now that in spite of such overwhelming evidence, even in one of the

---

* P. 27, l. 7.

† Mâtulagrahańenâtmabandhavo mâtŕibandhavaḱ pitŕibandhavaś cha yonisambaddhâ upalakshyante, te cha patnî duhitara ity atra darśitâḱ.

clearest cases possible, any law-court could nonsuit a claimant simply because the mass of proof which would have supported his right, was not accessible in English to the judge, appears to involve so anomalous a state of things that its continuance must be thought to be very undesirable.

The best and most efficient means of remedying it would of course be a thorough acquaintance of the Indian judges with the *original* text of the Hindu law literature, and their ability to examine for themselves in the original language all the texts which may have a bearing on a case before them. Nor need such a remedy be looked upon as chimerical; for the study of Sanskrit required for a legal training to this end would not imply more than the labour of a few years.

But as some time might have to elapse before this object could be attained, it is at least to be hoped that the most immediate wants pointed out in this paper will be provided for by the competent authorities.

A thorough revision of all the translations of Hindu law texts hitherto used in the Indian Courts should be undertaken at once, not in order to set them completely aside, but with the view of correcting their mistakes while preserving all that is good in them, and of harmonizing their quotation of the same texts so as to render the identification of the latter possible.

And, besides, the most important works, as yet accessible only in Sanskrit, should be translated into English, so that at least the whole of Yâjñavalkya's Code, with the Mitâksharâ, the Vîramitrodaya, some commentaries of Jîmûtavâhana's Dâyabhâga, some of Raghunandana's Tattvas, the Nirńayasindhu, the Dharmasindhusâra, the principal treatises on Śrâddha, impurity, and marriage, and those on adoption, should soon be within the reach of an English judge.

The study of Sanskrit is now so successfully pursued in India, and native scholarship has already given such excellent proof of its mastery both of Sanskrit and English, that with united efforts in India itself, there would be no difficulty, within a few years' time, in accomplishing this greatly needed work.

APPENDIX TO PAGE 18.

The oldest Hindu lawgivers lay down the rule that members of a united family have a joint community of worldly and spiritual interests. Hence, according to them, their income and expenditure is conjoint; they cannot individually accept or bestow gifts, or make loans; nor can they reciprocally bear testimony, or become sureties for one another; moreover, certain of their religious duties being undivided, one member of the family only is entitled and obliged to perform them for the rest. Accordingly, in doubtful cases it was held that partition of a family was proved, if it could be shown that all or any of these criteria of union were wanting. The requirements of an advancing civilization, however, led to a more definite explanation of this general rule. Trade, commerce, or similar causes, often compelling co-parceners to live away from home, or in different houses, the whole of their affairs could not be managed conjointly, nor could *all* their religious duties be performed in common. The difficulties, therefore, of determining from the criteria already alluded to whether a family was a divided or a united one, multiplied in time, and the works of Colebrooke, Strange, Macnaghten, and Grady very justly dwell on them.* A more recent work, however, that by Mr. R. West and Dr. J. G. Bühler,† is not satisfied with admitting, as its predecessors had done, that there are difficulties which must be dealt with according to their merits and as they arise; it summarily rejects *all* the criteria or 'signs of separation,' mentioned by the native authorities, as inconclusive, and consequently as devoid of value in a legal sense.

"The will of the united co-parceners to effect a separation," the Editors

---

* See Mr. Standish Grove Grady's 'Treatise on the Hindoo Law of Inheritance' (1869), where, in Sec. ix., pp. 415 ff., on 'Evidence of Partition,' all that relates to this subject is very carefully collected. See also the 'Manual of Hindu Law,' by the same learned author (1871), Sec. ix., pp. 273 ff.

† A Digest of Hindu Law; from the replies of the Shastris in the several Courts of the Bombay Presidency. Book II. Partition. Bombay, 1869. As this work reached me after the foregoing paper had been read to the East India Association, the translation of the chapter of the Vîramitrodaya "On a woman's separate property," contained in its Appendix (pp. 67 ff.), was then unknown to me, and has to be added to the translation of Hindu Law Texts enumerated at pp. 5 and 6.

of this Digest say,* "may be (1) stated explicitly; (2) or implied. As to express will it may be evidenced by documents or by declarations before witnesses . . . ." And "as to implied will," they continue,† "the Hindu authors are prolix in their discussions of the circumstances, from which separation or union may be inferred. According to them the 'signs' of separation are:—(*a*) the possession of separate shares; (*b*) living and dining apart; (*c*) commission of acts incompatible with a state of union, such as trading with or lending money to each other, or separately to third parties, mutual gifts or suretyship. They add also giving evidence for each other, but from this in the present day no inference can be deduced. (*d*) The separate performance of religious ceremonies, *i.e.* of the daily Vaiśvadeva, or food-oblation in the fire préceding the morning-meal; of the Naivedya, or food-oblation placed before the tutelary deity; of the two daily morning and evening burnt-offerings; of the Śrâddhas, or funeral oblations to the parents' manes, &c." The Editors then add: "None of these signs of separation can be regarded as, by itself, conclusive"; and again they say:‡ "As no one of the marks of partition above enumerated can be considered conclusive, so neither can it be said that any particular assemblage of these alone will prove partition. It is in every case a question of fact to be determined like other questions of fact, upon the whole of the evidence adduced, circumstantial evidence being sufficient."

But here it must first be asked what the Editors of this Digest call 'evidence' in addition to that admitted by them as such under the head of "express will"? For, if none of the evidence afforded by the 'signs of separation,'—whether this evidence be taken by itself or combined,—can, as they assert, establish a proof of partition, what evidence is there left but "documents" or "declarations before witnesses"?§ Yet as denial of separation, and litigation ensuing on it, will rarely occur when the party interested in the denial knows that his opponent is in possession of a partition deed, or can produce witnesses before whom the intention to separate has been formally declared, and as under such circumstances it will offer no difficulty to a judge, while, on the other hand, the cases presenting a real difficulty will just be those in which no documentary or other evidence of a similar nature exists,—it is hard to appreciate the value of the advice which the Editors afford in their last quoted words. But as the most striking part of their statement consists in the summary rejection, as legal proof, of all and each of the "signs of separa-

* Introduction, p. xii.

† P. xiii.

‡ P. xv.

§ P. xii.

tion,"—whereas some of these are so strongly relied upon by the native authorities, and have been so cautiously spoken of by Colebrooke, Strange, Grady, and other European writers of eminence,—it will not be inexpedient to inquire whether in this matter a judge may henceforth feel entitled to dispense with a knowledge of all that is stated on this point in Hindu works, and simply content himself with endorsing the opinion of the Editors of the Bombay Digest.

One of the most prominent "signs of separation," as we have seen, is based on religious grounds. It concerns the joint or separate performance of certain religious rites, some of which are mentioned in the quotation just given from the Bombay Digest. In regard to the legal irrelevance of these, the Editors of this Digest even grow emphatic. "The separate performance of the Vaiśvadeva sacrifice, of Śrâddhas and other religious rites," they say,* "is still less conclusive," viz. than the "living and dining apart" previously spoken of and declared by them to be "not conclusive of the fact" of separation. They seem to arrive at this inference from the interrogatory connected with a case to which they refer, and from a passage of a native authority to which they point, as forming part of their remarks on this case.

The case is that reported by them at p. 58. It gave rise, on the part of the Court, to the following amongst other questions: "He [viz. the son of an elder wife] was in the habit of performing the sacrifice called Vaiśvadeva on his own account. Should he be considered a separated member of the family? and can any man whose food is cooked separately perform the ceremony, or is it a sign of separation?" Upon which the Pańḍit so questioned replied:† "Those members of a family who individually perform the ceremonies of Vaiśvadeva and Kuladharma, and have signed a Fârikhat, may be considered separated. It does not appear from the Shastras that the elder son of a person is obliged to perform the Vaiśvadeva on his own account, although his father and step-brother are united in interests and he himself lives and cooks his food separately in the same town without receiving the share of his ancestral property. A person may, however, perform the ceremony by the permission of his father."

On this reply of the Pańḍit the Editors again observe:‡ "The Shastri is right in not considering the separate performance of the Vaiśvadeva as a certain sign of 'partition,' though it is enumerated in the Smṛitis among these signs. The general custom is, in the present day, that even undivided coparceners, who take their meals separately,

* P. xiv. † P. 59. ‡ P. 60.

perform this ceremony, at least once every day, each for himself, because it is considered to purify the food." But here it may be observed that all the Paṅḍit really said was, that when a man lives and cooks his food apart from his father and stepbrother who are united, it does not appear from the Shastras that he is *obliged* to perform the Vaiśvadeva on his own account; and what follows therefore from his words is, that if, living apart from his relatives, he *were* obliged to perform the Vaiśvadeva, such an *obligation* would prove that there was *no union* between him and the relatives named. The real drift of his answer, therefore, was not to show, as the Editors suppose, that the separate performance of the Vaiśvadeva was *in no case* a "certain sign of partition," but to recommend to the Court the investigation of the fact whether the person in question was or was not "*obliged*" to perform this ceremony separately from his relatives.

In a note on the word Vaiśvadeva the Editors had previously said* that "this ceremony is performed for the sanctification of food before dinner," and after the words above quoted (". . . . . because it is considered to purify the food"), they continue: "We subjoin a passage on this point from the *Dharmasindhu*:† (Dharm. f. 90, p. 2, l. 3 and 6 Bombay lith. ed.): *juhuyât sarpishâbhyaktair grihye 'gnau laukike 'pi vâ, yasminn agnau pached annaṁ tasmin homo vidhîyate. Avibhaktânâm pâkabhede prithag vaiśvadevaḥ kṛitâkṛita iti bhaṭṭojîye;* 'Rice mixed with clarified butter should be offered in the sacred domestic fire, or in a common fire. The oblations (at the Vaiśvadeva) should be made in that fire, with which the food is cooked . . . . Bhaṭṭojîdîkshita declares that, if members of an undivided family prepare their food separately, the Vaiśvadeva-offering may be performed separately (in each household) or not."

Their remark, however, regarding the purpose of the Vaiśvadeva, as well as their quotation from the Dharmasindhusâra and their translation of it, are very inaccurate. For, as will presently be seen, the Dharmasindhusâra states that the object of the Vaiśvadeva is the consecration of one's self *and* of the food; whereas the Mitâksharâ, in commenting on Yâjñavalkya, I., v. 103, altogether contests the doctrine that the V. is intended for the consecration of the food, and after some discussion on this theory, arrives at the conclusion that it solely concerns the (spiritual) benefit of the person performing it. And as in quoting from the Dharmasindhusâra the Editors in the beginning of the passage alleged

---

* P. 59.

† An abbreviation, by the Editors, of *Dharmasindhusâra*, which is the full name of the work meant, by *Kâśînâtha*.

have left out half a verse which *essentially* belongs to it, while before the words ascribed to Bhaťťoji they have omitted another *material* portion of the text, their translation is not only incorrect, but the very ground on which the author of the Dharmasindhusâra adduced Bhaťťoji, has been misunderstood by them.* But even supposing that all the remarks of the Editors on the Vaiśvadeva were correct, they would still not prove anything in respect of the legal inconclusiveness of "Srâddhas and other religious rites," all of which are included in their sweeping assertion which sets these rites aside for the purpose of legal evidence.

As the object of this paper, however, is not to correct the mistakes of any individual writer, but to show how necessary it is that a judge should examine for himself all that the native authorities teach in regard to questions that may come before him, and how the very replies of even the most learned Paňdits may be conducive to fallacies—since the correctness of a reply mainly depends on the correctness and pertinence of the question put, — I will, as an illustration of the difficulties which beset this subject, add a translation of a few passages from three works only, since even these will clearly prove that the bearing of the performance of certain religious ceremonies on the question of union or division cannot be dispatched in the offhand manner implied in the ruling of the Bombay Digest.

In treating of the daily religious duties of a Hindu the *Dharmasindhusâra* under the heading 'on the duty of the fifth division' (of a day divided into eight parts) contains the following passage: †

"The Vaiśvadeva is to be performed for the removal of (sins committed in) the five *Sûnâs*. The five *Sûnâs* are the five places where injury may be done (to living beings); viz. the wooden mortar in which grain is threshed; the stone slab on which condiments, &c., are ground with a muller; a fire-place; a water-jar, and a broom.‡ The commencement of

---

* The essential words omitted before '*juhuyât*' are: gṙihapakvahavishyânnais tailakshârâdivarjitaiḱ, (*juhuyât*, &c.); and those which should have preceded, and are absolutely required at the quotation '*avibhaktânâm*, &c.,' from Bhaťťoji, read: sa châyaḿ vaiśvadeva âtmasaḿskârârtho 'nnasaḿskârârthaś cha; tenâvibhaktânâḿ pâkaikye pṙithag vaiśvadevo na, vibhaktânâḿ tu pâkaikye 'pi havishyântareňa pṙithag eva, (*avibhaktânâm*, &c.) For the translation of the whole passage, see p. 37, ll. 10 ff.

† Dharmas., ed. Bombay (1861), III. A., fol. 95 *b*, ll. 7 ff.

‡ The object of the Vaiśvadeva is similarly defined in a passage of Śâtâtapa quoted in Raghunandana's Âhnikatattva (ed. Calc. 1834, vol. i., p. 251); and the five Sûnâs are frequently alluded to, *e.g.* in Manu, III., 68, Śankarâchârya's comm. on the Bhagavadgîtâ, III., 13, and they are also defined in Ânandagiri's and Śrîdharasvâmin's gloss on the latter.

the Vaiśvadeva is early (*i. e.* in the morning), not like that of the Agnihotra, late (*i. e.* in the evening); accordingly the resolve to perform it, as expressed in the words: "early and late, the Vaiśvadeva (should be performed")).* The five great sacraments are to be performed day by day; and these are the sacrament of the Veda, that of the gods, that of created beings, that of the manes, and that of men.† The sacrament of the Veda has been already explained.‡ Those who follow the ritual of the Ṙig-veda consider that the Vaiśvadeva consists of the three sacraments of the gods, created beings, and manes. The sacrament of men is the giving food to men. An oblation of food cooked in the house and fit for sacrificial purposes,§ free from sesamum-oil, factitious salt, and such like

---

* From *Raghunandana* (vol. i., p. 250) and similar works it results that the proper time for the performance of the V. is always during the day, and that the evening performance of this ceremony is permitted only under special conditions, as for instance when 'cooking' takes place for the entertainment of a guest. Some authorities, moreover, absolutely forbid the *repetition* of the ceremony on the same day, whether by day time or in the evening. But compare p. 39, l. 15.

† These five *mahâyajñas*, 'great sacrifices' or 'great sacraments,' are mentioned in the oldest works, *e. g.* in the Śatapatha-Brâhmańa (XI., 5, 6, 1)—also quoted from this Brâhmańa in Śrîdatta's Âchâradarśa—; in Manu, I., 112, &c., Yâjñavalkya, I., 102, &c.—*Manu* (III., 70) defines them as follows: "teaching (which, according to Kullûka, includes reading, viz. the Vedas) is the sacrament of the Veda; offering rice &c. or water is the sacrament of the manes; an oblation (of food) in fire is the sacrament of the gods; presentation of food (viz. throwing ghee or rice, or the like, in the open air) to created beings, is the sacrament of created beings; hospitality is the sacrament of men."

‡ Viz. in a preceding portion of the text, here not translated.

§ Substances, called *havishya*, or fit for sacrificial purposes, are frequently mentioned in ritual works, as in the Kâtyâyana Śrauta Sûtras (VII., 2, 2), or in works dealing with ritual matters, as in Manu, Yâjñavalkya, &c. The *Mitâksharâ* in its comment on *Yâjñ.*, I., 239, names as such: rice of different varieties, barley, wheat, kidney-beans of two varieties (phaseolus mungo and phaseolus radiatus), wild grain (wild roots, or in general such food as forms the diet of an ascetic), a black potherb called *kâlaśâka*, *mahâśalka* [explained as a kind of fish; Wils.: a prawn or shrimp], cardamoms, ginger, black pepper, asafœtida, molasses, candied sugar, camphor, rock-salt, sea-salt, bread-fruit, cocoanut, the plants called *kadalî* and *badara*, the produce of a cow,—viz. milk, curds, butter, or other preparations made of her milk,—honey, flesh, &c. On the other hand, as substances unfit for sacrificial oblations the *Mitâksharâ* names: *kodrava* (paspalum kora), *masûra* (ervum hirsutum), chick-pea, *kulattha* (dolichos biflorus), pulâka, a legume called *nishpâva*, a kind of bean called *râjamâsha* (dolichos catjang), the white pumpkin gourd, two kinds of the egg-plant (*vârttâku* and *vŕihatî*), *upodikâ* (basella rubra), the (unsacrificial substances), and dressed with ghee, one should make in the (sacred) domestic fire, or the ordinary fire; (for) the law ordains that such an oblation (should be made) in the fire with which a man cooks his food.* Since the Śrâddha occurring at fixed periods is performed by (performing) the sacrament of the manes included in the Vaiśvadeva ceremony, no entertainment of Brâhmans takes place (as it would) on behalf of the Śrâddha occurring at fixed periods. And since also the Śrâddha, (due) on the day of new-moon, is performed by (performing) it (viz. the sacrament of the manes), Bhaṫṫoji says, that those who are unable to perform the Śrâddha, due on the day of new-moon (regularly), should do so once (at least) in the course of a year. In the case of (impurity arising from) childbirth, the rule is that the five great sacraments are dropped. And this Vaiśvadeva is performed for the sake of one's own consecration and that of the food.† Therefore amongst members of a united family when they cook (their food) in common, a separate performance of the Vaiśvadeva (by each member) is not (allowed); but amongst members of a divided family, even when they cook (their food) in common, the Vaiśvadeva (must be performed) separately (by each of them) with some sort of substance fit for sacrificial purposes. According to Bhaṫṫoji, amongst members of a united family, when the cooking (of their food) does not take place in common, the Vaiśvadeva may be performed separately or not.‡ When no cooking (of food) takes place on the eleventh and

---

shoot of a bamboo, longpepper, orris root, *Śatapushpâ* (anethum sowa), saline earth, ordure, factitious salt, a buffalo's-chounri, her milk,—curds, —butter, or other produce of buffalo's milk; &c.—Compare also on the same subject Manu, III., vv. 266 ff., the Vishńu-Purâńa, Book III., ch. 16; the *Nirńayasindhu*, I., fol. 13; *Raghunandana*, vol. i., pp. 70, 142 and 250; *Śrîdatta's Âchâradarśa* (Benares, 1864), fol. 56 *a*; &c.

* The Âchâradarśa (fol. 56 *a*) which quotes a passage to the same effect from Angiras, regarding the sacred and ordinary fire, adds: "the sense of this passage is: a man who maintains a sacred fire should cook his food and make the oblation, in this (sacred) domestic fire; one who does not maintain such a fire, in the ordinary fire."

† See p. 35, ll. 31 ff.

‡ The words "*an oblation of food cooked in the house, &c.*" (p. 37, ll. 10 ff.) till "*performed separately or not,*" are the complete passage, represented in the Bombay Digest by the words "*rice mixed*" till "performed *separately (in each household) or not*" (see above, p. 35, l. 21–l. 27). The correctness of the last words "performed separately or not" might at first sight seem doubtful, since their value in Sanskrit is the compound *kṙitâkṙita*, and this word (according to Páń., II., 1, 60, not a Dvandva, but a Karmadhâraya) would literally mean 'done—not done,' *i. e.* 'imperfectly done,' or 'done as if not done,' *i. e.* 'done in vain.' That in the

similar days (of abstinence), the Vaiśvadeva should be performed with grain (esp. of rice), milk, curds, ghee, fruits, water, and the like substances. Let a man perform it with rice and so on, (throwing such substances) with his hand,—or with water, (throwing the latter) with his hollowed palms, into water; but let him at the performance of the Vaiśvadeva avoid *kodrava* (paspalum kora), chick-pea, the kidney-bean (phaseolus radiatus), *masûra* (ervum hirsutum), *kulattha* (dolichos biflorus), and all factitious salt called *kshâra* and *lavańa*. When a man lives abroad, the Vaiśvadeva should be performed at his house by the instrumentality of his son, priest, or other (proper substitute); and should there not be at his house such other (proper) agent he himself must perform it abroad. Those who conform to the ritual of the Ŕig- and Black-Yajur-vedas should perform it twice (a-day), according to the text which says: 'it should be performed by day and by night.' But if unable to do so, they may, at the same time, repeat it or perform (the day- and night Vaiśvadeva) together.* The usual practice of followers of these two Vedas is to cook their food and perform the Vaiśvadeva, in the ordinary fire."†

In the chapter treating of the religious duties of sons *whose father is alive*, the same work contains the following statement:‡

"Sons not separated from their father should not perform the Vaiśvadeva separately; for it is stated that 'one who lives upon the cooking of (*i. e.* the food cooked by) his brother, is (like) one who lives upon the cooking of (*i. e.* the food cooked by) his father.' Hence, if the father maintains a sacred fire, even when the cooking and the Vaiśvadeva are effected with the sacred fire, his unseparated sons, although they, too, maintain a sacred fire, should not perform the Vaiśvadeva separately. Those who think that, in the absence of cooking, a fire becomes an ordinary one, may cook merely in order to consecrate their fire. But by members of a divided family the Vaiśvadeva should be performed

---

quotation from Bhaťťoji, however, the word has not this sense, but the one given it in the translation of the Bombay Digest, and in that above, follows not only from the sense in which the word *kŕitâkŕita* is unmistakably used in other passages of the *Dharmasindhusâra* and *Nirńayasindhu* (since its meaning there becomes clear from the interpretations following it), but also from the injunction of *Âśvalâyana*, which is analogous to that of *Bhaťťoji* (see p. 41, ll. 21 ff.).

* See note * of page 37.

† There follows a description of the manner in which the V. is performed by members of the Vaishńava and other sects, of the rules relating to the *Naivedya* ceremony, and other detail which it is not requisite here to enter into.

‡ Bombay ed. (1861), III. B., fol. 3 *a*, ll. 8 ff.

separately (by each of them). And since (according to the followers of the Ṛigveda-ritual*) the Vaiśvadeva consists of the three daily sacraments, viz. those of the gods, created beings and manes, those (who entertain this doctrine regarding the Vaiśvadeva), even if their father is alive, will perform the (daily) sacrament of the manes, forming part of the five great (daily) sacraments. To the followers of the Black-Yajurveda, however, the five great (daily) sacraments are distinct from the Vaiśvadeva; they (consequently) perform the (daily) sacrament of the manes, if their father is alive, (only) when they are members of a divided family."

In the chapter treating of those entitled to perform the *Śrâddha*, the same work says:†

"The son of one's own body has the preferential duty (and right) to perform the annual and other Śrâddhas and the funeral ceremonies which take place immediately after death. If there are several such sons, the *eldest* has this duty (and right); on failure of him, or if he is not present, or if his right has lapsed through having become an outcast or similar (disqualifications), the eldest after him. The statement, however, (made elsewhere) that in the absence of the eldest the youngest has always this right, not the sons between them, is without authority. Hence, if sons live in a state of division, the *eldest*, after having received from the younger (brothers) the (necessary) property, should perform all the funeral rites up to that called Sapiṅḍana.‡ But the annual and other Śrâddhas each of them must perform separately. If, however, sons live in a state of union, even the annual and other Śrâddhas must be performed by one of them only. (Still) since what is done by one (member of a united family) accrues to the benefit of the rest, all the sons should keep such rules as the observance of chastity, the not touching another person's food,§ and similar ones. If sons do not live in the same place, whether they stay in different countries or in different houses, each of them should perform the annual and other Śrâddhas separately, even if they are members of an undivided family."‖

---

* See p. 37, ll. 7 ff.

† III. B., fol. 4 *a*, ll. 10 ff.

‡ That is, inclusive of the first sixteen Śrâddhas which end with the *Sapiṅḍana*, also called *Sapiṅḍîkaraṅa*.

§ *Yâjñavalkya,* III., 241, classes 'feeding on others' amongst the crimes, called *upapâtaka*, which are only a degree less than the *mahâpâtaka*, or most heinous offences. *Manu,* III., 104, foretells parasites that, after death, they will become the cattle of their hosts.

‖ The rest of this chapter regulates the rights of younger sons in the

In the important chapter on the Śrâddha itself, under the head of "*settled rules relating to members of a divided and an undivided family,*" the same work, after a general reference to previous statements, has the following:*

"Of brothers and other members of a family, divided in property, all the (religious) duties are separate. But that the funeral ceremonies and the sixteen Śrâddhas up to the Sapiṅḋana (which are performed during the first year after a death) should be performed by one of them only, has been already stated.† Yet if members of a family are undivided, all such acts as may be done without (spending any) property, *e. g.* bathing, the Sandhyâ-devotion, the sacrament (*i. e.* reading) of the Vedas, muttering of prayers, fasting, reading the Purâṅas, are done (by each of them) separately; whether such acts recur at regular periods, or are occasional, or (purely) voluntary; separately, also; such ceremonies of regular recurrence, enjoined by vedic or traditional works, as are performed with fire. Another view founded on the teaching of Kâtyâyana and others is, that 'one who lives on the cooking of a brother is (like) one who lives on that of a father.' Of the five great (daily) sacraments those of the gods, created beings, manes, and men‡ should be performed by the *eldest* (brother) only. If the cooking is done separately (by members of a united family) those who conform to the rules of Âśvalâyana, say that the separate performance of the Vaiśvadeva (by each member of such a family) is optional.§ Since, if the eldest (brother) does not perform the Vaiśvadeva, it is (the duty) of a younger (brother) to perfect the cooking (of the food by means of this ceremony), some enjoin that before eating, some of the food should be thrown by him into the fire, and some given to a Brâhman. The worship of the (tutelary) gods may be performed (by each of them) separately, or (by all of them) conjointly. The annual Śrâddhas, those performed on the day of new-moon, at the sun's entrance into a new sign, eclipses, and similar Śrâddhas should be performed by the eldest only. The Śrâddhas, also, performed in holy places (*e. g.* of the Ganges) and those of the same category should be performed by one member only of an undivided family, if all the members happen to be together (in the place), but separately, (by each member) if they happen to be in different places. The same rule applies

---

absence of the eldest, and in their absence those of other members of a family successively to perform the Śrâddhas. Its importance regarding the rights of inheritance, requires no remark; but as these rights do not concern the present paper, no further extract on this point is here given.

* III. B., fol. 37 *b*, ll. 5 ff.

† See p. 40, ll. 20 ff.

‡ See p. 37, ll. 4 ff.

§ Compare p. 38, ll. 20 ff.

to the Śrâddha, which is performed at (the holy city of) Gayâ (in Behar). As regards sacrificial ceremonies, at which voluntary gifts are made, and which can be effected only by means of (spending some of the family) property, the right of performing them depends on the assent of the brothers and other (members of the united family). The Śrâddha on the 13th day of the dark fortnight of the month Bhâdra, which is under the asterism Maghâ, it is stated, should be performed separately by each member (of an undivided family)." *

The work from which these passages are taken, is a compilation from other works, among which it prominently names the *Nirńayasindhu*, com-

* Compare for the Śrâddhas to be performed at holy places and the 13th of the dark fortnight of the month Bhâdra, also the following passages from Wilson's translation of the *Vishńu-Purâńa* (III., 14, vv. 17-19): "He who, after having offered food and libations to the Pitŕis, [manes] bathes in the Ganges, Satlaj, Vipâśâ (Beas), Sarasvatî, or the Gomatî at Naimisha, expiates all his sins. The Pitŕis also say: 'after having received satisfaction for a twelvemonth, we shall further derive gratification by libations offered, by our descendants, at some place of pilgrimage, at the end of the dark fortnight of Mâgha'"; and (*ibid.*, III., 16, vv. 17 ff): "In former times, O king of the earth, this song of the Pitŕis was heard by Ikshwâku, the son of Manu, in the groves of Kalâpa: 'Those of our descendants shall follow a righteous path, who shall reverently present us with cakes at Gayâ. May he be born in our race who shall give us, on the thirteenth of Bhâdrapada and Mâgha, milk, honey, and clarified butter." (Wilson's Works, vol. viii., pp. 170 and 197.) As pointed out by the editor, the phrase "for a twelvemonth" is in the Sanskrit text represented by *varshâmaghâ;* and the phrase "on the thirteenth of Bhâdrapada and Mâgha" by *trayodaśîm . . . . . . varshâsu cha maghâsu cha.* But the former being rendered by Śrîratnagarbha: *aparapakshamaghâtrayodaśî*, and the latter: *varshâsu, bhâdrapade, maghânakshatre trayodaśîm*, it would be better to substitute for them: "on the 13th day of the dark fortnight of the month Bhâdra, which is under the asterism Maghâ."—The sanctity of this day and its appropriateness for the performance of the Śrâddha already result from Manu, III., 273 and 274, where the *same* expression—*trayodaśîm . . . . . varshâsu cha maghâsu cha*' occurs, and is interpreted by Kullûka to v. 273: *varshâkâle maghâtrayodaśyâm*, and to v. 274: *bhâdrakŕishńatrayodaśî;* also from *Yâjñavalkya*, I., v. 260: where the words *varshâtrayodaśyâm maghâsu* are explained in the same manner by Vijñâneśvara: *bhâdrapadakŕishńatrayodaśyâm maghâyuktâyâm.*—Compare also Sir W. Jones, on the lunar year of the Hindus, As. Res., vol. iii., p. 292. Besides these verses, other quotations relating to the same subject, from *Śankha*, *Śâtâtapa*, and others, occur in Jîmût., III., 1, 18, in Raghunandana's Tithitattva (Calc. ed. 1834, vol. i., pp. 75, 160), in the Nirńayasindhu (II., fol. 42 *a*, *b*), Dharmas. (II., fol. 31 *b*), &c., which also show that each member of a family, whether divided or undivided, must for himself perform this particular Śrâddha.

posed by *Kamalâkara*, in the year 1611, P. C.* As the latter is held in especial esteem by the Mahrattas for whose benefit, it seems, the Bombay Digest was chiefly intended, I will add a translation of its chapter: "*On the settled rules relating to members of a divided and undivided family,*" which likewise forms part of its section on the Śrâddha.† It runs thus:

"The *Prithvîchandrodaya* quotes these words of *Marîchi*: 'If there are many sons of a father who live together, all that is done with the undivided (family-) property, by the eldest, the rest consenting, must be (considered as) done by all of them.' These words mean that, though the eldest is the agent, all of them share in the result (of his acts). Therefore such religious rules, as the observance of chastity, &c., must be kept by every one of them, since they consecrate the persons who obtain the result. And this applies also to re-united members of a family, on account of the analogy (that exists between them and members of a united family).‡

"The *Mitâksharâ* quotes these words of *Nârada*: 'The religious duty of unseparated brethren is single; when partition has been made, even the religious duties become separate for each of them.'§ *Vrihaspati* also says: 'Of members of a family who live (together and) cook (their food) in common, the sacraments of the manes, gods and twice-born should be single; of those who are divided, they should be performed in each house separately.'‖ Though in this last text, no exception being mentioned, the prohibition of a separate performance (of religious acts) in an undivided family would also (seem to) obtain for such acts as the reading of the Vedas, the Sandhyâ devotion and the like, it (nevertheless) merely relates to the performance of the Śrâddha, Vaiśvadeva and other ceremonies

---

* This date is given by the author himself at the end of his work, in the words: vasu (= 8) ŕitu (= 6) ŕitu (= 6) bhû (1) *i. e.* 1668 of the era of Vikramâditya.

† Ed. Bombay (1857), III. B., fol. 65 *a*, ll. 4 ff.

‡ This passage also occurs in the same chapter, fol. 8 *b*, ll. 11 ff.

§ Mit., ch. ii., sec. xii., § 3.—The same quotation also occurs in the *Vîramitrodaya*, Calc. ed., p. 169 *b*, 223 *a*; the *Vivâdachintâmańi* (ed. Calc. 1837), p. 162 (Colebrooke's translation of this passage in the Mit., and that of Tagore p. 311 in the Viv. materially differ from one another); in the *Smŕitichandrikâ* (Calc. 1870) p. 8, *Vyavahâramayûkha*, ch. iv., sec. vii., § 28 (Borradaile's translation being the same as Colebrooke's), and in other Digests.

‖ This quotation also occurs in the *Vivâdach.*, p. 125 (Tagore, p. 227); *Vîramitrodaya*, f. 172 *a*, 222 *b*; *Kullûka* to *Manu*, IX., 111; *Dâyakaumudî* (Calc. 1827), p. 28; *Smŕitichandrikâ*, p. 8; &c.

which can be effected only by (spending some of the family) property; for such property having more than one owner, one (member of the family alone) would not be entitled to spend it. All such acts, however, as may be done without (spending any) property, *e. g.* muttering prayers, fasting, the Sandhyâ devotion, reading the Vedas and Purâṅas, whether such acts recur at regular periods, or are occasional, or (purely) voluntary, each member is competent to perform separately (for himself). For there being no expenditure of property, no consent (of the rest) is required; and consequently the words (before quoted) 'with the undivided (family-) property' cannot apply to such acts. And this conclusion also results from the following text of *Âśvalâyana* as quoted in the *Prayogapârijâta:* 'Amongst twice-born men who cook (their food) in common there should always be separate the sacrament (or reading) of the Vedas, the Agnihotra, the worship of the gods, and the Sandhyâ devotion.' (In this passage) Agnihotra signifies such ceremonies of regular recurrence, enjoined by vedic or traditional works, as are performed with fire. For (the right of each member of a family to fulfil) these duties (separately) is logically analogous to the right acquired by the consent of the rest. The Śrâddha of the father, and other acts of regular recurrence which have the same consequence (for all the members of a family) a single (member) is entitled to perform even without the consent of the rest; for it is said:* 'Even a single (member) of a family may conclude a donation, mortgage, or sale, of immovable property, during a season of distress, for the sake of the family, and especially for pious purposes.' 'For pious purposes,' means, according to Vijñâneśvara,† for the performance of indispensable duties, viz. the Śrâddha of the father, or the like.

"But some maintain that even of members of an undivided family, if they cook (their food) separately, and if they stay in different countries, each has to perform separately (for himself) the Śrâddhas on the day of new-moon and the annual Śrâddhas; for *Hârîta* has said: 'If undivided brethren cook their food separately, each of them should also perform separately the Vaiśvadeva and the other Śrâddhas'; and *Yama:* 'If a son who is not separated (from the family) stays in a foreign country, he should perform (for himself) separately the Śrâddha of the father on the anniversary of his death, and the Śrâddha on the day of new-moon.'

---

* By *Vṛihaspati*, according to the Ratnâkara (as quoted by Colebrooke) on the *Mit.*, ch. i., sec. i., § 28. Comp. also the *Vîram.*, f. 181 *a*; *Vivâdach.*, p. 161.

† Mit., ch. i., sec. i., § 29.

"If (the drift of) these texts is properly considered, their sense (will be found to be) this: Of the five great (daily) sacraments, the eldest should with the consent of the other (members) of the family perform the sacraments of the gods, created beings, manes and men; for also *Vyâsa* has said: 'Food should never be eaten without previously making a sacrificial offering, and presenting a first (portion) of it (to a Brâhman); amongst members of an undivided or re-united family what is done even by a single (member) *is* done (by all).' But if one's food has been prepared without the eldest (member) having performed the Vaiśvadeva, he may eat it after having silently thrown some of it into the fire. For, where treating of the rights of members of an undivided family the *Prithvîchandrodaya* quotes this passage from *Gobhila*: 'Whose food in the family is first ready, he may eat it after having put a certain portion of it into the fire, and given a first (portion) of it to a Brâhman.' Again, *Âśvalâyana* mentions the ceremonies which (members of a divided family) should perform separately when they cook their food separately; and also separately when they cook it in common; (his words are):* 'Of members even of a divided family, if they live (together and) cook (their food) in common, one, the master (of the household), should perform the four (daily) sacraments which (in the order of the five †) are preceded by the sacrament of speech. But men of the twice-born classes, whether members of an undivided or a divided family, if they cook (their food) separately, should, previous to taking it, each separately perform these sacraments day by day.' The sacrament of the Veda, the Sandhyâ devotion, bathing, the sacrament of the manes, and the like ceremonies are for the reason stated, performed separately (by each member); but on account of the two texts quoted, the worship of the gods either in common (by one) or separately (by each member); the Śrâddhas on the day of new moon, at eclipses, &c., by one member only; the Śrâddha at holy places, and similar Śrâddhas by one only, if all the members of the undivided family happen to be together (in the place), but separately (by each member), if they happen to be in different places. And so likewise the Śrâddha which is performed at Gayâ. For *Hemâdri* quotes this passage from the *Kûrma-Purâńa*: 'Many well conducted and excellent sons must be wished for; (for) if one of their number goes to Gayâ, we are saved by him, and he enters upon the highest path.' ‡

---

* Compare the same passage in the subsequent extract from the Vyavahâramayûkha; p. 47, ll. 33 ff.

† See p. 37, ll. 4 ff.

‡ The first portion of this quotation ('many' till 'Gayâ') occurs

"As regards voluntary acts, such as sacrificial offerings connected with the making of gifts, and the like, the right of performing them depends on the assent of the other (members of the family); that of muttering prayers and performing similar acts which entail no expenditure of property exists without (such) assent. *Aparârka* quotes these words of *Paiťhînasi*: 'The annual and similar Śrâddhas should be performed separately by each member of a divided family; but if performed by one member of an undivided family, it is as good as if they were performed by all of them.' That the monthly Śrâddhas, which precede the annual Śrâddha, must be performed conjointly (by the whole family), *Laghu-Harîta* has declared in these words: 'The sixteen Śrâddhas which end with the Sapiṅďana, sons should not perform (each of them) separately; nor ever, even when divided in property.' The Sapiṅďana here implies a monthly Śrâddha; for this results from the words of *Vyâsa*: 'After the year (following the death of the father) the eldest (son) should perform the Śrâddha before the assembled family; but after the Sapiṅďana (has been accomplished) each son should perform it separately.' And *Uśanas* says: 'The 'new' *Śrâddha*,* the Sapiṅďana, and the sixteen Śrâddhas should be performed by one member of the family only, even if the latter is divided in property; but the Śrâddha on the 13th day of the dark fortnight of Bhâdra, which is under the asterism Maghâ † should be performed separately by each member even of an undivided family'; as has been already mentioned.‡ But when *Vriddha-Vasishťha* says, 'the monthly Śrâddha, the ceremony of setting a bull free, and the Sapiṅďana should be performed by the eldest, as well as the first annual Śrâddha',—his injunction is without authority. In the Pariśishťha of the Ṛigveda ritual (it is said that members of a family) should perform the 'new' Śrâddha conjointly."

With these extracts from the Dharmasindhusâra and its predecessor, the Nirṅayasindhu, it will now be expedient to compare the law on this matter as laid down by the principal authority of the Mahrattas, the *Vyavahâramayûkha*. It is contained in the following passage. §

---

with some variation in the Râmâyaṅa (ed. Bombay, 1861), II., 107, v. 13; and is quoted also by several treatises on adoption, the Dattakakaumudî, Dattakasiddhântamañjarî, &c.

* The 'new' Śrâddha (navaśrâddha) is the collective name of the ceremonies which begin on the first day after a death, and end on the tenth (comp. Dharmas., III. B., fol. 7 *b*, l. 9).

† *Maghâtrayodaśî*; see note * of page 42.

‡ Viz. III. B., f. 8 *b*, and f. 9 *a*, where the same quotations from *Laghu-Harîta* and *Uśanas* occur.

§ Ch. iv., sec. vii., § 28–§ 33. Consistently with the opinion ex-

"*Nârada* says: * 'The religious duty of unseparated brethren is single; when partition has been made, even the religious duties become separate for each of them.' Here the term 'unseparated' is intended to denote the chief topic (treated of), whilst 'brethren,' on account of its (merely) qualifying the former, is not to be taken in its literal sense. Therefore in an unseparated family, even if it consists of a father, grandfather, son, son's son, paternal uncle, brother, brother's son or other (relatives), their religious duty is single.

"Here again, though conjointness of an act, in regard to its various stages, follows as a logical consequence if there is sameness of place, time, agency, and so on, an express text would cause such conjointness to cease, if the agency is not the same, though (it is) that of members of an undivided family. Hence all those religious duties, enjoined by vedic and traditional works, which are fulfilled by means of fire, even of unseparated (brethren) are separate for each (of them), since they are different according as different kinds of fire would be connected (with the ceremony). Even so the Śrâddha of a paternal uncle, brother's son, &c., at the day of new moon and other (seasons) is separate by reason of the separation of the deified person (from the *pârvaṅa* rite); but the Śrâddha of brothers (dying) without (maintenance of) a sacred fire is performed by one and the same act, because all the deified persons are conjoint. Again, by residence abroad and the like (causes), there being a difference in the places (where members of a family live, the Śrâddhas are to be performed) separately (by each member); the ceremonies also performed with fire are separate for those who maintain a sacred fire. But the worship of the household deities, the Vaiśvadeva and similar ceremonies are performed (conjointly) by one and the same act. Hence *Śâkala* says: 'Of those who live (together and) cook (their food) in common, there is but one worshipping of the deity in the house, and but one Vaiśvadeva; in a family of divided brethren these acts are performed in each house separately.'

"As for the text, however, of Âśvalâyana, as quoted in the Pârijâta, which says: 'Of members even of a divided family, if they live (together and) cook (their food) in common, one, the master (of the household), should perform the four (daily) sacraments, which (in the

---

pressed at p. 31, in the translation that follows, as much as possible has been retained of Borradaile's version; several portions of the latter, however, had necessarily to be altered, as not correctly rendering the sense of the original.

* See p. 43, ll. 17 ff.

order of the five) are preceded by the sacrament of speech; but men of the twice-born classes whether members of an undivided or a divided family, if they cook (their food) separately, should, previous to taking it, each separately perform these sacraments day by day';*—this text has reference to members of a re-united family; for that such is its import, follows from the words 'of members even of a divided family, if they live (together and) cook (their food) in common,' and from the words 'whether members of an undivided or a divided family.'

"Therefore if there be a separate cooking of food, as is sometimes the case, amongst members of a re-united family, their great (daily) sacraments are separate. 'Sacrament of speech' is 'the sacrament (*i.e.* the reading) of the Veda.' The phrase 'those (sacraments) which are preceded by the sacrament of speech' is represented (in Sanskrit) by (one word which is) a Bahuvrîhi (or possessive) compound of the class where the quality expressed by it (as the predicate of something else) is not intended for *the* (*i. e.* the essential) quality (of the latter); for were this compound meant to convey such an (essential) quality, the words 'preceded by the sacrament of speech' would yield no sense, since there would then be no cause for excluding the first (sacrament); whereas it logically follows that the four (sacraments only) are here meant.†

---

* See p. 45, ll. 17 ff.

† The grammatical observation in this passage, relating to Bahuvrîhi compounds, is an allusion to a *paribhâshâ* or interpretation-rule which occurs in *Patañjali's Mahâbhâshya* on *Pâṅini*, I., 1, 27 (viz. the par. *bahuvrîhau tadguṅasaṁvijnânam api;* on which Nâgojîbhaṫṫa in the *Paribhâshenduśekhara* observes that, on account of the word *api*, it also implies *atadguṅasaṁvijnânam*). The drift of this *paribhâshâ*, as Patañjali explains it, is to show that Bahuvrîhi compounds (in English comparable to adjective compounds like lightfoot—*i. e.* one who possesses light feet,—or blueeye-d, &c.) are of two kinds, the one expressing a quality or an attribute which is essential, and the other expressing a quality or an attribute which is not essential, to the subject so predicated by the compound. Thus, as Patañjali illustrates, if you say: 'there march the priests having red turbans on,' the Bahuvrîhi *lohitoshṅîshâḣ* 'having red turbans on' implies here an essential quality of the priests, since this quality cannot be disconnected from their appearance as they march. But if you say: 'bring hither the man who possesses brindled cows (*chitragu*),' you want the man to be brought, but not his cows; hence the quality of 'possessing brindled cows' would in this case be disconnected from the appearance of the man, and therefore would not be essential to it. In the first instance the quality expressed by the compound was the characteristic feature, in the second it is merely the descriptive mark, of the subject predicated by it; and this, as *Nâgojî* in his commentary observes, depends on the sense. The application, then, regarding the compound

Hence the sacrament of the Veda should be performed separately (by each member of the family). But (after all) these two texts are not much respected by the learned.

"As regards, however, the following sentences in the *Dharmapravṛitti*:

'Sons unseparated must (conjointly) celebrate one anniversary Śrâddha for both parents; if they be in different countries they must (each of them) separately perform the Śrâddha on the day of new moon and the monthly Śrâddhas. If they go to (reside in) different villages, unseparated brethren should always (each of them) separately perform the Śrâddha on the day of new moon and the monthly Śrâddhas of both parents. When unseparated, but residing in different villages, each living upon the wealth acquired by himself, these brothers should celebrate the Pârvaṅa-Śrâddha separately;'

"And as regards the following passage in the *Smṛitisamuchchaya*:

'The Vaiśvadeva, the anniversary Śrâddha, as well as the Mahâlaya rite, in case the members of a family reside in different countries, are to be celebrated separately (by each of them), and in like manner the Śrâddha on the day of new moon,' —

"These (two) texts, some say, have reference to members of a re-united family residing in different countries. But the fact is that they have no authority.

"Or, to sum up: if there be sameness of place, time, agency and so on, conjointness (in the performance of the act) follows as a matter of logical reasoning. If the agency is not the same, such conjointness (only exists if it) is established by an express text. If the place is not the same, some base (the rule concerning) the separate performance of Śrâddhas and other ceremonies on circumstantial reasoning, since in such a case there is neither a logical necessity nor an express text (which would establish conjointness)."

Even from these few extracts it will be seen that commensality or the reverse of it has not been regarded as a proof of either union or division of a family; for without any restriction whatever, as we find,

---

vâgyajñapûrvaka, 'preceded by the sacrament of speech,' which our text makes of this paribhâshâ is: that if this predicate of the 'four sacraments' spoken of had been considered by the writer as *essential* to them, the four sacraments would have been represented by him as accompanied and headed by 'the sacrament of speech'—which would be nonsense. If, however, this predicate was understood by him as being merely a descriptive one, the sense would be, as it should be, that the four sacraments are those which in their usual order come after the sacrament of speech, but are not accompanied by it.

members of a *united* family are spoken of as residing and 'cooking' apart from one another, and members of a *divided* family as living and messing together.

And I may add at once that I know of no Hindu law-authority which *distinctly* declares that 'living or dining apart' is a legal *test* of partition. *Manu, Vyâsa,* and other lawgivers, it is true, sometimes say that sons and parents should 'live together,' but in the first place, the words they use to this effect, do not imply an obligation; they merely convey a recommendation or permission; and secondly, their expression 'living together' does not intimate a particular mode of life which would be a *test* of union, but is used synonymously with 'union' in general.

Hence, when *Manu* says:* "Either let them thus live together, or let them live apart (*Kullûka : i.e.* let them separate), if they have a desire of performing religious duties, &c."—his words merely express the lawfulness of both union and separation, but not a criterion of either. Or, when *Vyâsa* writes, "It is lawful that brothers and their parents, if the latter are alive, should live together," the *Smṙitichandrikâ,* after quoting these words, adds: "even after the demise of the father brothers live together for the sake of increasing mutually their property; for *Śankha* and *Likhita* have said 'Let them willingly live together, for being in harmony and united they will become prosperous.' "† Here again, therefore, 'living together' does not imply a particular mode of domestic life, without which union could not exist, but simply a state of union in general as contrasted with a state of separation in general. And consequently, passages of this kind are not alleged by the Digests under the head of "*evidence of partition,*" but in the chapter treating of the *periods* of partition;—a distinction, which, from a Hindu point of view, is very material.

There is indeed one text which might seem to imply that "*cooking apart*" (not living apart) *was* considered by a native authority as a sign of partition, viz. a passage in Nârada's Dharmaśâstra,‡ for it occurs there under the head of "ascertainment of a contested partition," and being quoted in Jîmûtavâhana's Dâyabhâga under the same head, has been translated by Colebrooke thus:

"Gift and acceptance of gift, cattle, grain, house, land and attendants

---

* IX., 111; in the Vyavahâra-Mâdhavîya quoted as a verse of *Prajâpati.* Compare also Jîmûtav. Dâyabh., I., § 37.

† Ed. Calc., p. 8.

‡ J. O. MS. No. 1300, fol. 38, *b*: dânagrahańapaśvannagṙihakshetraparigrahâh́, vibhaktânâḿ pṙithag jñeyâh́ pâkadharmâgamavyayâh́.

must be considered as distinct among separated brethren, as also *diet*, religious duties, income and expenditure."*

But in consulting the explanation given by the best commentators of this passage, and in comparing it with the sense put upon it in other Digests, it will be found that instead of "as also diet, religious duties, income and expenditure," the translation should most probably run: "as also *the religious duties connected with the cooking* (of food), income and expenditure"—when the very omission of 'cooking apart' in this passage would strongly confirm the opinion just expressed.†

---

* XIV., § 7.—The italics of *diet* are mine.—In Colebrooke's Digest of Hindu Law, vol. iii., p. 407 and p. 417, this passage is translated thus: "When co-heirs have made a partition (distribution) the acts of giving and receiving cattle, grain, houses, land, household establishments, dressing victuals, religious duties, income and expenses are to be considered as separate, and (conversely) as proofs of a partition;" whereupon Jagannâtha observes (p. 407): "'dressing victuals' [here means] for the service of guests and the like, and for the food of the family; 'religious duties'; the aggregate of constant and occasional acts of religion." It will be seen however from the next note that his interpretation of *pâkadharma* is not borne out by the principal commentators of Jîm. Dâyabh. and the other Digests.

† On the first part of the compound *pâkadharmâgamavyayâń*, Achyutânanda, in Bharatachandraśiromańi's edition of Jîmûtav. Dâyabh. (p. 357) comments: *pâkadharmâ vaiśvadevadharmâdayań*, when pâkadharma, therefore, would not be a Dvandva, but a Tatpurusha compound; and similarly *Śrîkŕishńat.*: (as also in the previous Calc. editions) *pâkadharmo vaiśvadevâdikarma*, i. e. "religious duties connected with cooking, that is, the Vaiśvadeva duties (or ceremonies), and similar ones"; *Râmabhadra* in the edition named merely comments on *dharma* (not on *pâkadharma*), viz. *dharmo daivapitrâdikarma;* but as *daiva* is frequently used synonymously with *vaiśvadeva*, the meaning of his words would be: "the Vaiśvadeva, the sacrament of the manes, and similar ceremonies"; when it becomes probable that the proper reading should be *pâkadharmo daiva°*, or that *dharma* is abbreviated by the commentator for *pâkadharma;* in the *Vîramitrodaya* also (p. 223 *a*, l. 12) where the same passage of Nârada is quoted, *Mitramiśra* explains (l. 14) *dharmo vaiśvadevâdiń, ekapâkena vasatâm iti prâguktavachanât*, i. e. "religious duty means the Vaiśvadeva and so on, on account of the previous quotation (from Nârada) which says: 'of those who live (together and) cook (in common) (the worship of the manes, gods and twice-born should be single, &c.)' "; where *dharma* is therefore used in the sense of *pâkadharma*, and the 'sign' in question is not the 'cooking,' but the religious rites connected with the cooking.—Again in the *Vivâdachintâmańi*, where the same passage occurs (p. 162) *Vâchaspatimiśra* likewise takes pâkadharma for a Tatpurusha; viz. *pâkadharmań pârvańâdiń*, "the religious duties connected with cooking, i. e. the Pârvańa and other ceremonies." In the

It is to be presumed that on the strength of this passage,—as translated by Colebrooke,—Strange, Macnaghten, and other modern authors, even though rejecting non-commensality as a 'sign' of separation, allowed it a place amongst the different kinds of 'evidence of partition;'* but with the aid of the printed texts and commentaries we now possess, there can be no doubt that we should not be justified in stating for certain, as the Bombay Digest does, that *according to Hindu authors*, living and dining apart is a *sign* of separation.†

But though the extracts already adduced merely confirm the negative inference derivable from the ancient law authorities, that commensality, taken by itself, affords no legal evidence regarding the state of a family, they show us that a different view must be entertained of the value which some ceremonies at least possess for testing doubtful cases of this kind.

Some religious acts, as we see, must, according to all authorities, be performed separately by each member of a family, and others in

---

Dâyakaumudî, too, (p. 278) *Śrîkŕishńat.'s* commentary on this passage, as already mentioned, is quoted and adopted by Râmajayatarkâlaṁkâra. On the other hand in the *Vyavahâramâdhavîya* and *Vyavahâramayûkha* (IV., 7, § 34), instead of *pâkadharmâgama°*, the text reads *dânadharmâgama°*, when *Nîlakanťha* explains *dânadharmo lekhyâdiḱ*, "the duties connected with *gifts*, i. e. written deeds, and the like."—The word *grain* which occurs in Colebrooke's translation represents the Sanskrit *anna;* and lest any inference be drawn from it regarding 'diet,' or lest it be doubted that this is the proper sense of the word as here used, I may mention that the *Dâyakaumudî*, on the authority of the *Vivâdabhangârńava*, says: "*anna* here means 'the getting of grain,'" and adds: "but some say *anna* here means 'buying corn, grain, &c., for the sake of food (*annârtham*).'" But even for *anna*, the Vivâdach. has the v. l. *artha* and explains it with *arthotpâdana* 'producing wealth.'—Whatever view therefore we may take of this passage it is clear that the balance of probability is in favour of Śrîkŕishńatarkâlaṁkâra's, Achyutânanda's, and Vâchaspatimiśra's gloss, and that *Nârada*, if he really wrote *pâkadharma°* and not *dânadharma*, did not make 'cooking,' but the religious duties connected with it, 'a sign of partition.'

* Macnaghten, for instance, in his 'Principles of Hindu Law' (Madras, 1865), p. 53, says: "It (viz. partition) cannot always be inferred from the manner in which the brethren live, as they may reside apparently in a state of union, and yet, in matters of property, each may be separate; while, on the other hand, they may reside apart, and yet may be in a state of union with respect to property: though it undoubtedly is one among the presumptive proofs to which recourse may be had, in a case of uncertainty, to determine whether a family be united or separate in regard to acquisitions and property."—Similarly, 'Strange, Hindu Law,' vol. i., p. 229.

† See p. 33, ll. 5, 6.

common, whether the members of such a family live in a state of union or separation. Thus, the reading of the Vedas, muttering prayers, and in general all religious acts which entail no expenditure, must be performed separately by each member even of a united family; on the other hand, the sixteen Śrâddhas which occur during the first year after a father's death, must be performed in common,—that is, as a rule, by the eldest son on behalf of the whole family—even if the latter is a divided one. Hence the performance of acts or ceremonies like these is no criterion either way, whether of union or separation. Yet we find that if members of a united family 'cook' their food in common, they are bound to perform, conjointly, the four daily sacraments of the gods, manes, created beings and men, the anniversary Śrâddha, the Śrâddha on the day of new moon, and the Śrâddhas of this category, the Tîrtha-, Gayâ-, and Śrâddhas of this nature, whilst, if messing apart or if separated, they would be bound to perform these rites separately, each for himself. The *Vaiśvadeva* also, members of a separated family *must*, and members of a united family, if not messing together, *may*, perform separately; but members of a united family, if messing together, *must* perform it conjointly. Hence, if it can be shown that relatives *mess together*, and yet perform all or any of these ceremonies *separately*, each for himself, it is clear that, on the ground of all authoritative texts, a case of division is made out.

Again, it is expressly enjoined that a voluntary religious ceremony entailing expenditure can be performed by a single member of a united family only on the condition that the rest of the family allow him to do so; and to this clause no restriction is attached regarding commensality or living apart. Hence if it can be shown that a person performed such a ceremony without any protest on the part of his relatives, yet without having obtained their consent, such evidence would prove that he was divided from them; or, conversely, if it can be shown that he asked and obtained the consent of his family to perform such a ceremony, proof is afforded that at that time he was a member of a united family.*

Some statements, therefore, of Sir T. Strange, on this subject are liable to objection. For, though he was right in dividing the religious

* How great the amount of evidence available on this purely religious ground is, can be fully ascertained only from the ritual works; but an inference to this end may be obtained from Colebrooke's Essays 'On the Religious Ceremonies of the Hindus,' and particularly from that relating to the Śrâddha (Miscellaneous Essays, vol. i., pp. 123 ff.); also from H. H. Wilson's 'Religious Practices and Opinions of the Hindus' (Works, vol. ii., pp. 40 ff.; edited by Dr. R. Rost).

duties of a Hindu into such as are "indispensable," and others which "in their nature are voluntary,"* he was mistaken in assigning to the latter class "consecrations, the stated oblations at noon or evening with whatever else there may be of a similar kind, the performance or non-performance of which respects the individual merely." And he was likewise mistaken when he said that "the proof in question [viz. of partition] results from the separate solemnization of such [rites], the acquittal or neglect of which is attended with consequences beneficial, or otherwise, to the individual, in his capacity as housekeeper (gṙihastha), or master of a family, the third and most important order among the Hindoos; of this kind are among others, the five great sacraments, in favour of "the divine sages, the manes, the gods, the spirits, and guests."† For we have seen that each member even of a united family must for himself perform several such ceremonies if the members of that family 'cook' apart from one another. And when he added, "Still such separate performance is not conclusive; it is a circumstance merely,"—we must point to the cases above mentioned, in which it *is* conclusive, provided the members of a family mess together. Again, exception must also be taken to the remark which the same learned author appended to a Paṅḋit's answer touching the same question.‡ "Had the division been doubtful," he said, "then certainly the joint performance of the ceremonies would be a conclusion against it; a conclusion merely, however; or, as it has been appositely called in another case, 'a token' (*adyuharana*, I suppose, in the original) not a proof." For, one of the ceremonies here alluded to is "the annual ceremony for a father," and the joint performance of such a ceremony, as we have seen, can only take place in a united family. The usual words for 'token,' moreover, from which he inferred that it implies a conclusion only, are in Sanskrit *chihna* and *lakshaṅa*, and each is often used in the sense of "characteristic or essential mark," when it is tantamount to proof.

The Editors of the Digest, however, not merely repeat, as we have seen, the general, and on account of its generality, objectionable statement of Strange, but after the words above quoted § add: "In the pre-

---

* Hindu Law (1830), vol. i., pp. 227 ff.

† Those explained in note † of p. 37 are here meant.

‡ Hindu Law, vol. ii., p. 392.

§ P. xiv. "The separate performance of the Vaiśvadeva sacrifice, of Śrâddhas and other religious rites, is still less conclusive. At Dig. chapter iv., Q. 4, infra, a passage of Bhaṫṫojîdîkshita is quoted, according to which coparceners, living apart, may or may not perform the Vaiśvadeva each for himself, and, in the present condition of Hindu society, &c." See p. 34, ll. 12 ff.

sent condition of Hindu society, the performance of all religious rites has become so lax and irregular as to afford no safe ground for inference." I do not know on what authority this sweeping assertion is made, for the Editors do not at all indicate the source whence it has been derived. Hitherto the most reliable accounts of the present religious condition of India seem to lead to the conclusion, supported also by the writings of Colebrooke, Wilson, Haug, and others, that there is still in the country a very large proportion of the community which very tenaciously clings to what it considers its orthodox faith, and that this community is extremely jealous of allowing any European to pry into its devotions and to become acquainted with the detail of them. Nor is it clear what the Editors call 'lax and irregular;' for, compared to the vedic ritual, for instance, that taught by the Purâńas may be so qualified, and judged by the standard of the latter, doubtless more recent ceremonies may likewise be thus termed. A statement so vague and general is in reality therefore meaningless, for it neither specifies the ceremonies to which it relates, nor the period or the standard by which to obtain a medium of comparison between the present and past. Yet even if the Editors had afforded us the information required, and if their statement concerning the quality of the actual worship of the Hindus were in some sense correct, it still appears that their conclusion would not be borne out by it. For in so far as the Hindu law of inheritance appeals to evidence based on religious grounds, it is quite immaterial whether the detail in the performance of this or any other ceremony concerned by it, agrees with the teaching of the ancient or mediæval, or even modern ritual—provided such a performance is held, rightly or wrongly, to be in the spirit of the orthodox faith. Whether, therefore, the Śrâddhas or the Vaiśvadeva, for instance, are now performed in strict accordance with the ritual relied upon by Colebrooke in his 'Essay on the Religious Ceremonies of the Hindus,' or not, is for *legal* purposes absolutely irrelevant, so long as the popular mind still believes that the Śrâddha benefits the soul of a deceased relative, or that the Vaiśvadeva removes the sins which a man may have committed in preparing his daily meals. And that this belief no longer exists, the Editors would still have to prove. It is certain, moreover, that the Law Courts of the Bombay Presidency and the Pańdits can entertain no doubts in this respect, for otherwise it would be unintelligible why in suits relating to inheritance, the judges should address questions to the Pańdits about the performance of Śrâddha and other rites, and that the Pańdits should strengthen their replies by a reference to their doctrinal works; and even the Bombay Digest reports three instances, at least, of such interrogatories, at pp. 48, 57, and 58. It would be a mistake, therefore, on the part of an Indian judge were he to adopt the inference suggested to him by the Bombay Digest that no performance of any religious ceremony whatever can afford conclusive evidence regarding the union or division of a Hindu family, and in consequence, that henceforth he may dispense with a study of the native authoritative works concerned in this matter. Even the few data here collected, by way of illustration, will sufficiently show that in doubtful cases these works will still be his safest guide.